[H.A.S.C. No. 114–61]

GAME CHANGERS—UNDERSEA WARFARE

HEARING

BEFORE THE

SUBCOMMITTEE ON SEAPOWER AND PROJECTION FORCES

OF THE

COMMITTEE ON ARMED SERVICES HOUSE OF REPRESENTATIVES

ONE HUNDRED FOURTEENTH CONGRESS

FIRST SESSION

HEARING HELD
OCTOBER 27, 2015

U.S. GOVERNMENT PUBLISHING OFFICE

97–495   WASHINGTON : 2016

CONTENTS

GAME CHANGERS—UNDERSEA WARFARE

House of Representatives,
Committee on Armed Services,
Subcommittee on Seapower and Projection Forces,
Washington, DC, Tuesday, October 27, 2015.

The subcommittee met, pursuant to call, at 2:45 p.m., in room 2118, Rayburn House Office Building, Hon. J. Randy Forbes (chairman of the subcommittee) presiding.

OPENING STATEMENT OF HON. J. RANDY FORBES, A REPRESENTATIVE FROM VIRGINIA, CHAIRMAN, SUBCOMMITTEE ON SEAPOWER AND PROJECTION FORCES

Mr. FORBES. As the members of this subcommittee and our witnesses are well aware, America's ability to project power overseas is currently being challenged by the rapid growth of other nations' military forces and the fielding of novel capabilities that undermine our freedom of maneuver and action and threaten to deprive our Nation of the many benefits we derive from our command of the seas. If we remain on our present trajectory, I fear we may see our seapower and power projection capabilities eclipsed and our influence eroded in critical regions overseas.

In the past, Congress has responded to similar threats by undertaking great expansions of our air and maritime forces. Championed by legislators like Carl Vinson, these buildups reenergized American seapower and projection forces and sustained them for another generation.

Given the challenges and constraints we face today, however, I believe a different response from Congress and the Pentagon is required. Building more things will be part of the solution, but it is my belief that what we really need at present are new things, innovative capabilities and concepts that will, quote, "change the game" in the many areas of military competition where the trends are unfavorable.

Today this subcommittee kicks off a series of hearings examining potentially game-changing concepts and capabilities with a look at the undersea domain. This is a domain in which the United States has for decades been dominant and benefited immensely from it. Our superiority in this domain has enabled the United States to collect sensitive intelligence, hold at risk foreign fleets, attack targets on land without warning, and maintain the secure second-strike capability that is essential for deterrence.

While surface ships and forces ashore are coming under increased threat from anti-access/area-denial [A2/AD] capabilities and being forced to operate at longer ranges, U.S. submarines still enjoy freedom of maneuver and the ability to operate with near impunity under the sea. In the view of many respected defense leaders and analysts, this provides an enduring strategic advantage that the United States should leverage to offset competitors' growing strength in other areas.

Unfortunately, as with so many elements of our fleet, the demand for undersea forces currently exceeds the supply, and the situation is forecasted to grow worse. At present, the U.S. submarine fleet is able to meet only 65 percent of commanders' requests for forces. Under current plans, the Navy's submarine fleet will shrink by 25 percent between now and 2030, with our fleet of attack submarines shrinking from 53 to 41 boats. Over that same period, we stand to lose 60 percent of our undersea payload capacity as our four SSGNs [cruise missile submarines] are retired from service.

So, at a time when our submarine force will likely be called upon to do more than ever, it is also going to be at its smallest size since World War II. At the same time, our existing sensors and weapons should be expected to decline in effectiveness as our adversaries' own capabilities improve.

Fortunately, the submarine community is aware of the challenges and opportunities it faces, and we are privileged to have two of its leading thinkers here before us to discuss them: Retired Vice Admiral Michael J. Connor, former commander of Submarine Forces—Admiral, thank you for being here today—and Mr. Bryan Clark, senior fellow at the Center for Strategic and Budgetary Assessments [CSBA].

Bryan, thank you for joining us.

These two submariners have been at the forefront of undersea innovation, and I am eager to hear from them as to what new undersea concepts and capabilities the Navy is currently developing and what more might be done to sustain and exploit our dominance in that critically important domain.

And, with that, I turn to another leading proponent of America's undersea power, our ranking member, Mr. Joe Courtney of Connecticut.

[The prepared statement of Mr. Forbes can be found in the Appendix on page 33.]

STATEMENT OF HON. JOE COURTNEY, A REPRESENTATIVE FROM CONNECTICUT, RANKING MEMBER, SUBCOMMITTEE ON SEAPOWER AND PROJECTION FORCES

Mr. COURTNEY. Thank you, Mr. Chairman.

I have a statement, which, again, I am going to have introduced into the record, and just really summarize really quickly by saying, you know, over the last 7 or 8 years, with the help of both of our witnesses here, you know, we actually, I think, have sort of reasserted the priority of our undersea force, kick-starting the *Virginia*-class production program to two a year, getting the design work on track for the *Ohio* Replacement Program. The *Virginia* Payload Module [VPM], which the chairman referred to, is, you know, filling a critical payload gap which is going to occur when the SSGNs go offline.

But the fact is we still have other challenges ahead of us, as I think we will hear from the witnesses. You know, the rest of the world has not sort of stayed frozen in the post-Cold War era. And, again, we can't have two better witnesses to sort of walk us through about where, you know, this committee should be focused in terms of trying to have a force multiplier to fill those gaps that the chairman referred to in terms of the combatant command [COCOM] and its requests, which are not going to be met, and that is probably going to get a little tougher as the fleet size declines in the next few years or so, and really trying to get, again, Congress focused on this, just like we were able to with the *Virginia* program and with the *Ohio* Replacement Program.

And that is really, I think, the purpose of this hearing. And hopefully we are going to get some good ideas in terms of ways we can improve, you know, our budgeting and authorization process to make sure that, again, we just don't lose that, you know, incredibly important edge that our country has in terms of the undersea domain.

So, again, I want to thank both witnesses for being here today, and particularly Admiral Connor, who is now, you know, back where he belongs, in southeastern Connecticut, and, obviously, though, here today still helping our Nation.

So, with that, I will yield back, Mr. Chairman.

[The prepared statement of Mr. Courtney can be found in the Appendix on page 35.]

Mr. FORBES. Joe, thank you.

And one of the things that we often say for opening statements is we tell our witnesses: You don't need to read your opening statement. You can make it a part of the record and just talk to us.

But today I want to emphasize how important both of these opening statements are. They are two of the best that I have read in a long time. And we are going to be encouraging our subcommittee members to read both of your statements, because I think they were just both excellent. So I thank you for the thought that you put into those statements and for the ideas contained in there.

And I encourage anybody today who hasn't read them to make sure you get a copy and read the full text that both of these gentlemen have put in their statements, because they are both excellent.

And, with that, Admiral Connor, I think we are going to start off with you, and we would love to hear your thoughts and comments. And thank you once again for your service to our country and for being here today.

STATEMENT OF VADM MICHAEL J. CONNOR, USN (RET.), FORMER COMMANDER, SUBMARINE FORCES

Admiral CONNOR. Well, thank you, Chairman Forbes, Congressman Courtney, and, really, all the members of the committee and staff. I would like to just briefly thank you for the support that I saw very clearly during my tenure as commander of the submarine force, as this committee reversed the decline of the submarine force, got us back to two a year, and has us—although the numbers will go down for a while, you stabilized the situation.

And it is your long-term commitment to Navy shipbuilding that is allowing things like the *Virginia*-class program to deliver such high-quality submarines ahead of schedule and under budget. It is because we have a fairly predictable future. Thank you for that.

I have a few suggestions. They are contained in my statement that I have submitted for the record. I will summarize them here.

The first point is that, while we talk about game-changing capabilities, many of which come in the form of vehicles, manned and unmanned and so forth and things we called payloads, it is important to keep in mind that those game-changing capabilities rest on the foundation of superior platforms that give us an operational advantage when we go head-to-head with the adversary. And the things that we bring to bear after that tend, in many cases, to leverage that capability. And it is a very important part. The other capabilities are not standalone.

The first point I want to make is that, in the game-changing capability, we need to start thinking in terms of range—range of weapons that we deliver under the water and above the water. It is important from the perspective that, as we look forward into a world where we present asymmetric challenges to our adversaries, that we take our superior platforms and then extend the range at which they can impart their effects across the theater. That is a true quandary for our adversaries, when they know that a submarine, for example, that they cannot detect has the ability to strike on short notice across a very wide area.

So, in the area of torpedoes, we are looking at, as the Navy restarts heavyweight torpedo production, they do that with a mind to increase the range of those weapons and then increase the ability to communicate with those weapons when they are far, far from the ship that launched them, even to the point where another aircraft or satellite relay may actually determine the final homing of that weapon.

The next point is that we need to get back into the business of submarine-delivered anti-ship missiles that can strike at very long ranges. This presents a huge quandary for our adversaries, who have to maintain an air defense posture if they are concerned that there might be a submarine in the area even if they can tell that there are no surface ships in the area. That is a true tax on their system. It changes their weapon load-out, it changes their radar posture, and it significantly helps our ability to track them.

The next point is, as we look at how in this world going forward where we have many, many commitments to know what is going on under the water in more areas than ever before, we have to change the way that we do that. We have to shift from relying on a small number of highly capable but fairly relatively expensive platforms to do it in a much more pervasive way with large numbers of smaller, less expensive things.

The good news is that the technology that we have today will allow us to do that. The advancements that have been made in robotics and autonomy and propulsion, in harvesting ocean power, have opened the door for those who are creative to make major, major improvements in how we sense what is going on in the ocean.

And my last major point is that, if we are going to leverage this type of opportunity, we have to be able to move much faster in the future on the technological front than we did in the past. And we will certainly need the help of the Congress in doing that.

We live in a world where the technology cycle is about 2 to 3 years long, and we also live in a world today with a typical program cycle, from inception of idea to funding and production, that can be 3 to 5 to 7 years. We cannot live in that world and keep pace with the technology of today. We will need your help in that, and we can talk about that later.

That summarizes my statement. I am ready for your questions, Chairman.

[The prepared statement of Admiral Connor can be found in the Appendix on page 37.]

Mr. FORBES. Admiral, thank you so much.

And, Mr. Clark, you are not a stranger to this subcommittee. We thank you for being here again and look forward to your comments.

And, with that, we yield you the floor.

STATEMENT OF BRYAN CLARK, SENIOR FELLOW, CENTER FOR STRATEGIC AND BUDGETARY ASSESSMENTS

Mr. CLARK. Thank you, Chairman Forbes and Congressman Courtney, for inviting me to testify today. And I am honored to be here with Admiral Connor, who is my former boss and a visionary leader in undersea warfare. It is truly a great honor for me to be here with him today.

This is a terrific topic for the first in the series of game-changing warfare area examinations, because today undersea warfare is something that the United States depends upon fundamentally for a lot of its war plans and a lot of its defense strategies as our way to get access to places that enemies with growing anti-access capabilities want to keep us out of. So we have to be able to sustain our level of dominance that we currently have in the undersea.

That dominance is likely to be challenged here in the coming years, with the advent of new technologies and the advent of more visionist powers. And you have heard of deployments of Russian submarines out of their normal bastions or out of their normal local areas, deployments of Russian ships that are, you know, potentially looking at undersea cables, and the growing Chinese submarine fleet.

So, clearly, there are competitors to the United States in the undersea domain that are going to look to take advantage of emerging technologies to establish their own capabilities to either deny us the ability to use the undersea or to use it to their own advantage.

So we can look at opportunities here, some game-changing opportunities, to sustain our undersea advantage that we enjoy today and then to, going forward, establish an enduring advantage against those new competitors.

I think there are three major areas where these technological changes are coming that our adversaries might be able to leverage, with the leveling of the technological playing field, but that we can also take advantage of ourself and that we need to.

The first one is new capabilities to detect submarines and also in technologies that would prevent detection of submarines. So you will see a competition ensue between detection and counter-detection, which wouldn't be dissimilar to what we see above the water when it comes to radar and electronic warfare that we are sort of familiar with.

The second area is in the power and autonomy of unmanned systems, so unmanned undersea vehicles as well as unmanned systems that you would deploy on the sea floor, like sensors or modules that would contain weapons and other payloads.

The third major area—and this gets to something Admiral Connor just talked about—is in the area of payloads, so in the kinds of things that you would carry on an undersea platform or on a ship that would deploy things undersea, so advancements in communications technology for under the water, advancements in the capability of weapons to be able to go long distances and to also be able to find targets undersea, and then also in the ability of these systems to communicate with one another and network with one another and coordinate their operations undersea.

So those three main areas of technology development offer opportunities for us as well as to our adversaries. These new technologies, though, will not make the oceans transparent in the near term or anytime in the future, probably, and they are not going to erode our dominance overnight. So we can take advantage of this time period in which we still have the advantage to invest in them.

What we need to do is—or just some key features of this future competition that are likely to occur are six major areas, so what I think we are going to end up with as a new basis for submarine detection that is going to emerge out of these sets of game-changing technology.

So we are used to passive sonar being the primary means by which we detect a submarine. So we listen under water, a submarine makes noise, we detect that noise and go attack the submarine. Well, as submarines have become quieter, that has become less possible. And, also, as adversaries have tried to develop their own anti-submarine warfare [ASW] capabilities, they are moving into new areas like active sonar and getting away from the idea of listening for the submarine and, instead, just using active sonar to bounce sound off of a submarine.

So that is going to create new requirements for the U.S. to be able to protect their submarines from detection. That is going to create a counter-ASW competition, and so that is something that we can look at both gaining advantage in and being able to use against our enemies.

We are also going to see the advent of undersea families of systems, or undersea systems of systems, where you have submarines and unmanned systems both on the sea floor and mobile ones, like unmanned vehicles, working with one another, communicating with one another to accomplish a mission, not dissimilar from how you see aircraft today.

So, today, with integrated fire control systems, you see an AWACS [Airborne Warning and Control System] aircraft being able to find targets and then direct fighter aircraft to go intercept those targets. You will see a similar emergence in the undersea, where manned platforms and unmanned platforms are going to be interacting in these families-of-systems constructs.

We are going to see probably the advent of seabed warfare, where the ability to find things underwater becomes very important and the ability to install them or remove them becomes very important, and whoever can do that better than the other competitor is likely to gain an advantage going forward. And you can see that even right now with the efforts the Russians are taking to try to identify and locate undersea cables.

And the last feature of this competition you are likely to see is the focus on cost imposition rather than attrition. So our normal model of warfare is we try to destroy the other guy's forces, kill as many of his people as possible, break as much of his stuff as possible. In the undersea, it is different because it is very hard to find things undersea, it is very hard to close the kill chain to destroy them. And so, as a result, you are going to see efforts to try to just impose costs on the enemy, force them to be always on the defensive, as Admiral Connor said, rather than trying to kill them outright. So we can look for ways to take advantage of that as the U.S., as opposed to that being used against us.

Some things that the Navy should do to take advantage of the technologies that are available and get ahead in this next phase of competition are five main things.

So first is to sustain and expand our submarine capacity. Because, as you noted, Congressman Forbes, we are going to have a reduction in overall submarine capacity here in the coming years where it is just actually going to go below the Navy's identified requirement of 48, and then we are also going to have the reduction in overall capacity with the retirement of the SSGNs. So looking at ways to be able to mitigate that reduction in overall submarine capacity will be important.

We need to achieve organizational alignment in the development of our undersea systems. Today, it is sort of a letting-all-the-flowers-grow effort, where we try to let everything come up and see which of these undersea systems, like an unmanned system or a sensor, is going to show promise. And, instead, we need to be a little bit more focused about how we manage and structure that effort.

We need to ensure that the new SSBN [ballistic missile submarine] will be survivable in an environment where new ASW methods, new submarine-detection methods are becoming common. And looking out 50 years or more into the future for that new SSBN, it is going to be hard to figure out what is the new ASW technique of the future going to be, but we have to have that determination and make those systems part of that submarine.

We need to establish priorities for unmanned underwater vehicle design and where they should be focused, for example, what mission should they be focused on and what sizes and capabilities do they need to have, as opposed to kind of the bottom-up approach that is proceeding today.

We need to look at how we evolve our SSNs [attack submarines] for new roles. Our attack submarines are going to be the heart of this undersea family of systems, so they need to be equipped and have the payload capacity to do so. So things like the *Virginia* Payload Module are very important. Maybe that should be part of every *Virginia*-class submarine in Block V rather than simply half of them.

And then the last thing is moving undersea systems from the research and development [R&D] community into acquisition. Because today a lot of these systems are languishing, waiting to transition into acquisition programs because of a lack of requirements or a lack of organizational wherewithal to push them across the "valley of death" and become something that is actually fielded as part of the fleet rather than an experiment that is done once or twice and looks good but never actually becomes part of our overall approach to undersea warfare.

So, in conclusion, I would say that the undersea—you know, America can certainly sustain its undersea advantage and impose costs on its enemies using the undersea, but we have to evolve our approach and evolve the capabilities that we are developing to be able to take advantage of the technologies that are emerging and be able to do that in the future.

Thank you.

[The prepared statement of Mr. Clark can be found in the Appendix on page 46.]

Mr. FORBES. Thank you, Mr. Clark.

And to our witnesses, again, thank you for being here.

This subcommittee is one of the most bipartisan subcommittees in Congress. And while we go outside these doors, we maybe differ on a lot of different things, we may be parochial in nature, we may have other issues, when we come in here, we are pretty much Team USA, you know, in how we do the best that we can do to defend and protect the United States of America.

One of the things I want to encourage subcommittee members to do—and Mr. Courtney and I both concur in this—for those of you who might have gotten here after our opening, we normally don't emphasize that you read the opening remarks. You can do that if you want to or not. These are two of the best opening comments that I think Joe and I both have seen in a long time that really outline this area. So I would just encourage all of our members to read those two opening remarks in their entirety.

And, as I look at those, to both of you, we are oftentimes tasked with looking at charts of platforms. And so we can look at number of SSBNs we have, how many we need, we can look at the *Virginia* attack subs, how many we need, how we are going to compare, look at our surface ships.

But, as I look at both of your written testimony as well as what you have verbally stated here today, it seems like what you are talking about in the future is we are going to have to, instead of just building more subs, which is important that we do, we are going to have to create these systems of systems that you talk about so that the subs that we have can be multiplied, not by having more subs only but by having systems that expand their both capacity and capability, I guess, in doing that.

And two of the problems that we have—Mr. Connor, you specifically outlined these in your written testimony. But we are going to have to be on the innovative edge if we do that. And innovation sometimes means coming up with the ideas but also being able to get to those ideas.

And the two concepts that I thought were pretty intriguing that you put out was, first of all, just with our normal budget process, it takes a year for one of our services to come up with their budget, and then it takes a year, on a good year, for us to be able to match that budget and get it to the President. And by that time, often-times the shelf life of the innovation has run out.

So I think both of you are concurring that we have to find, as to the innovation piece, how we do that faster. And so we would look, one, for your ideas on that, maybe an elaboration on that.

But the second thing—and I thought this is something we need to really look at too—is the concept of failure. We have developed a culture now where, if we fail, any platform, it is like the most horrendous thing that has ever taken place. And I think, Admiral, your thoughts on that would be, if we are not failing, we are not innovating. And you point out in your testimony that in Silicon Valley they are going to have a 90 percent failure rate. So even if we had a 50 percent failure rate, that is not a bad thing.

So I was wondering if the two of you could just kind of give us your thoughts on those concepts.

Admiral CONNOR. I would be happy to, Chairman.

And you described the limitations of the budget process very well. Even some of the tools that we have used to overcome the process, so to speak—we have a program we call Speed to Fleet, which behind closed doors we call the NBA [National Basketball Association] playoffs because what happens is that, over the course of a year, we compete various technologies within the Navy to decide which ones will get funded in the next budget. And the problem with even that is that is a year-long process, to do your fast project. It just doesn't make sense.

So, to a certain degree, I think the Congress and then whoever they select within the Department of Defense [DOD] to administer the program would have to create and oversee very much a venture-capital-like approach to innovation. The money has to be set aside. The money should be invested in projects that have credibility, that people can demonstrate why they have credibility. There ought to be milestones involved in that process, where people come back and show that they are on track and harvesting the results or making the progress that they intended to make—or not.

And the "or not" piece comes into your failure rate you talked about. And if something seemed like a good idea but the physics don't work out or the concept of operations is untenable, then there may come a point in some of the applications when we just say that this isn't working, we are going to stop, we are going to file the lessons away, and we are going to learn from it, but we are going to stop here and put that money where it can move us forward faster.

That may seem like a start-and-go-type process, but, at the end of the day, if you look at the way that works in other arenas, you make more forward progress by being bolder and making more bold attempts, even when you have occasional or even frequent failure in the process.

Mr. CLARK. So I would have two things that the Congress could do, potentially.

So one would be related to how do you incentivize the research organizations with regard to the things they pursue?

Today, research organizations in the Department are incentivized to transition things into the warfighters' hands. So they are graded on how well the projects they pursue end up turning into an acquisition program, or at least part of an acquisition program. Even an organization like DARPA [Defense Advanced Research Projects Agency] feels pressure to transition more capabilities into the warfighters' hands.

What that does, though, is it makes them, over time, shift from a focus on bold, innovative, game-changing ideas to things that are more evolutionary and less disruptive and more likely to turn into an operational capability that will turn into an acquisition program.

So one thing the Congress could do would be to incentivize a focus within these organizations, particularly the DARPAs and the S&T [science and technology] organizations, on more disruptive ideas that are more revolutionary. And so this comes to, how do we report this?

So the reporting requirements for technology programs are generally: How well did they transition? What is the percentage of transition? And then how fast did they transition? Things that take too long or things that don't transition are not rewarded, and things that do are rewarded.

If instead we ask and there are reporting requirements to say, characterize how your technology programs were in terms of how disruptive they were to the status quo in terms of technologies and how revolutionary were their operating concepts, that would be a way to incentivize organizations to move in the direction that they should be, which is bolder ideas that are going to be able to change the way we operate more dramatically than potentially just coming up with evolutionary changes that simply move the ball a little bit further down the field.

And I am thinking mostly of a DARPA-type model here. DARPA should be incentivized to pursue those game-changing technologies, but today they feel like they need to transition things to the warfighter, and, as a result, you are seeing a dulling of that focus on game-changing technologies.

So that is one thing, in terms of how do we—you know, we can incentivize them through reporting requirements and through driving them to take more risk and accept more failure in terms of how the Congress deals with these organizations.

I would say that the second thing is, in terms of getting the new capabilities more quickly into the warfighters' hands, because of the budget process and this 2-year delay that you discussed, maybe we should formalize an opportunity during the development of the appropriations and authorizations bills for the Department to come back and make changes, in consultation and coordination with Congress, to accommodate the fact that certain programs in those 2 years may have shown a lot of promise and should get more money, but, you know, our budget has been in stasis for the last 2 years. So we don't have that opportunity until the budget has been issued and a reprogramming is conducted.

So, instead of waiting for that reprogramming, change that appropriation while the appropriations bill is being developed over here on the Hill. It gives the Department a second opportunity to make changes to those small technology programs, some of which may have failed in the ensuing year and a half or some of which have shown great promise and need to be fostered further.

Mr. FORBES. Well, thank you both. And our subcommittee is going be looking to both of you two as we go down the road, perhaps, to laser in on some of these changes that we can do. We heard in the full committee just earlier today that one of the difficulties we have is a lack of competition now. So they said, before, a lot of our innovation came from the fact that the loser would create the innovation for the next time, and today we don't have that situation. So this is something I think is very, very important as we move forward.

Mr. Courtney is recognized for any questions he may have.

Mr. COURTNEY. Thank you, Mr. Chairman.

And, again, I just want to reiterate your comments about the testimony. Again, I just think it is—I would really encourage all the members and, frankly, the whole committee to take a look at it. Because, you know, clearly, the sort of post-Cold War holiday in the undersea realm is over, and, you know, the world is changing. And you guys really focused on it, you know, just in a really important way. So thank you, to both of you.

Mr. Clark, you talked a little bit about the *Virginia* Payload Module program, which, again, is right before us—actually, it is in the budget—in the authorization this year. At this point, again, it doesn't look like it is going to commence until 2019——

Mr. CLARK. Right.

Mr. COURTNEY [continuing]. With Block V. Again, the Navy shipbuilding plan, though, as you noted, is for only one out of the two a year *Virginia* classes, to incorporate that.

I mean, given the fact that—I mean, it is clear we are not only just talking about strike capability but also, you know, the family of systems, as you said. I mean, should we be looking at maybe trying to modify that proposal to, again, maximize the benefit of that modification?

Mr. CLARK. Definitely.

If you look at the cost of the Block V *Virginia*-class submarine with the VPM, it is going to cost less, in constant-year dollars, than the original Block III cost because of the cost savings that have been incorporated into the program through the design-for-affordability efforts and by the other efforts that EB [Electric Boat] and HII [Huntington Ingalls Industries] have taken to reduce the cost of building the ship. And you can see that in how fast they build them and how early they are completed. That translates into lower costs.

So the submarines are going to cost less money than their predecessors while offering more capability. So we should take advantage of that opportunity and expand the number that we are purchasing, because we need this capacity not just to replace the SSGNs, as you noted, for their strike capacity but also to enable these submarines to be the host and coordination platforms going into the future.

Because the model we have to start thinking of for the submarine is less of the tactical aircraft that goes into harm's way alone and unafraid and more like the aircraft carrier model, where it is the centerpiece of a family of systems that are operating in conjunction with it, some of which would come from the platform itself, and some may come from somewhere else. But that payload capacity is essential to afford it the ability to be that aircraft carrier of the undersea.

Mr. COURTNEY. And, Admiral Connor, again, you devised this undersea dominance campaign. If we have non-VPM *Virginia*-class subs versus those with the module, I mean, can you just talk a little bit about, you know, what the difference would be in terms of trying to implement that plan?

Admiral CONNOR. Congressman, I would be happy to do that.

The first point I would like to make is that it is a lot easier to be building subs in parallel that are exactly the same than to be having two variants coming off the line depending on what time of year it is because there are nuances there. So there are efficiencies that I believe would show up in production that probably aren't reflected in the way we calculate costs ahead of time.

The other issue, though, is, as we look to a world where we will intentionally pursue a path with a wide range of technologies—numerous less expensive technologies that we solve hard problems with numbers of small things—having the capacity built in place to deploy and retrieve things, even things that we haven't invented yet, would be a very important part of our strategic planning.

While we work in a timeframe probably with payloads and vehicles that become obsolete in 3 to 5 years, we have to plan on ships that are around for 30 to 40 years. And to make decisions today that would discount their ability to handle a wider range of payloads, I think, is worth reconsidering.

Mr. COURTNEY. And your comments about anti-ship missiles, I mean, again, that also sort of fits into the *Virginia* payload, you know, capacity, just to have more——

Admiral CONNOR. Very much so. If you just would take, you know, the typical range of a Tomahawk missile today, which I think you all know, and say that were an anti-ship missile, and you would draw a radius around a submarine operating undetected in some part of the world, and the fact that that ship could impose a mission kill on pretty much anyone they chose, using technology that exists in other missile areas today and applying it to a missile that we know we can fly off a submarine, that is a pretty huge quandary, as I said, for the adversary.

So the more capacity you have to employ those types of things, at the same time that you have these other payload options for sensing and so forth, would be critical.

Mr. COURTNEY. Great.

Thank you to both of you.

I yield back.

Mr. FORBES. Mr. Clark, did you have a——

Mr. CLARK. One thing I would add to that, too, on the payload capacity, what is really important is some people might argue that, well, if I try to use an anti-ship missile like the Tomahawk to attack a high-end destroyer of the Chinese, they will probably shoot it down. And I would argue that, well, if I shoot 10 or 12 Tomahawks at them, they may not shoot all of them down; all it takes is one to get through.

That would be a very good cost tradeoff. If I am paying for 10 or 12 Tomahawks at about a million dollars apiece to destroy a

$1.5 billion or $2 billion Chinese destroyer, that would be a good tradeoff to accept.

Mr. FORBES. Okay.

Mr. Wittman is recognized for 5 minutes.

Mr. WITTMAN. Thank you, Mr. Chairman.

Vice Admiral Connor and Mr. Clark, thanks so much for joining us today. Some interesting points about what we need to do to dominate in the undersea realm.

I want to expand from your concepts about using the submarine as kind of the centerpiece and having a number of systems that work in a dependence or in relation to the submarine itself, whether it is UUVs [unmanned underwater vehicles] or UAVs [unmanned aerial vehicles]. Great concept. I think the carrier strike group concept with the submarine is a great way to go about that. It lets us leverage an awful lot of different systems on different platforms and creates lots of uncertainty for our adversaries.

One thing, too, in a resource-restricted environment, which is where we are going to find ourselves, I think, at least now and into the foreseeable future, is we see our adversaries not only use nuclear-powered submarines, but we also see them use diesel-powered submarines.

Give us your perspective about us having a fleet with some of those other platforms, a diesel-powered submarine. I think the technology is there, and we can build those for half the price of nuclear submarines. Nuclear submarines certainly have a place, but the question is, our adversaries have significant numerical advantage, and, as the saying goes, quantity has a quality all its own.

What do we do, in looking at the ever-expanding numbers of our adversaries? And is there a place for diesel submarines as a platform, to look at something that is in addition to UUVs and UAVs, as we create these undersea systems?

Admiral CONNOR. Congressman, I have studied this issue a fair amount. I have been both the submarine commander and the anti-submarine commander in the Western Pacific, Arabian Gulf, and the Atlantic, and these are the types of things that I thought about every day.

What I found is the argument that suggested that the quantity of diesel submarines is a quality all its own is true if and only if the theater of operations is very constrained. And what you can do if you are the anti-submarine commander and the adversary is a diesel or even a diesel with air-independent propulsion capability, the energy density they have just isn't there. They can't move, on average, more than about 100 miles a day without resorting to coming shallow and operating their engines and therefore exposing themselves.

So I would contend that while a diesel submarine does not replace a nuclear submarine, because we can go much further, much faster at quiet speeds, a capable unmanned vehicle, I think, does fulfill that role of getting numbers in a relatively constrained area.

So we should be looking at sort of a high-low mix of capable submarines that can project a threat anywhere we want in a short period of time with the ability to deploy from submarines or other platforms—airplanes and surface ships—vehicles that can fulfill that mission that others use their diesel submarines for.

Mr. WITTMAN. As we look at the innovation and creation that takes place—and I agree with both of all of you, it takes place at a breakneck pace, and the current system of acquisition—and we talked about this earlier today—isn't well-suited to get technology to the warfighter quickly.

Give us some of your perspectives—and you shed a little bit of light on that in your testimony, but give us your perspectives on what we could do to really enhance that. You know, it is great to have a fund, but there is always this accountability side about what are you doing, who is going to oversee that, and those sorts of things.

But give us your thoughts about, first of all, how would you do that internally? How would you encourage the private sector to take that innovation, to develop it, to make it available to DOD? And if it is applicable, we can put it to use. If not, then there should be some ownership, I am sure, by the private sector.

But, anyway, give us your perspective on how we can make that happen.

Admiral CONNOR. The ability of the private sector to invest and to retain their intellectual property and profit from it when they succeed would be a huge incentive to bringing many companies that are not traditionally pursuing defense work into that arena. And there are some very innovative people who would be happy to spend their own money for a chance to compete. So that is one point.

The other area is probably more on the side of the Department than the Congress, but that is, when programs are defined, I think we have had a tendency to define them too narrowly. And sometimes that works in the favor of preservation of the program in the form it was conceived. But to the extent to which we could expand the definition of a program such that when good ideas happen that meet the intent of the program they can be incorporated.

If you want to see a good example of that, you could look at the Advanced Processor Build/Technological Insertion program we use on submarines, which—basically, we assume that the hardware becomes obsolete every 5 to 6 years and the software becomes out of date every 2 [years], so we plan for those changes. We could do similar things with hardware.

Mr. WITTMAN. Thank you, Mr. Chairman. I yield back.

Mr. FORBES. And, Admiral, just to clarify your response to Mr. Wittman, as I understand, you are saying if you had to spend defense dollars, you would rather have a limited number of very high-end platforms supplemented by a large number of more inexpensive, perhaps unmanned platforms, rather than putting it all in multiple midrange submarines. Is that a fair representation?

Admiral CONNOR. That is very accurate. I might say massive numbers of small platform.

Mr. FORBES. Right. That is great.

The gentlelady from Florida, Ms. Graham, is recognized for 5 minutes.

Ms. GRAHAM. Thank you, Mr. Chairman.

Thank you, Admiral, Mr. Clark. Appreciate you all being here.

I represent north Florida, where the Naval Support Activity Center in Panama City is located. Much of what we are discussing here today is being developed and tested there. As a matter of fact, there are commercial entities that are on the cutting edge of innovation.

I am curious about what you all are seeing in terms of our adversaries across the world and where they are in terms of developing unmanned undersea technology. Because, often, the challenges that we face are what drive development and drive the desire to be competitive in this area.

So, if you could speak to that, I would appreciate it.

Admiral CONNOR. The cutting edge of unmanned undersea today exists probably in the academic world and in the oil and gas exploration world. And they are developing a lot of technology very rapidly.

From what I have seen—and I am now out of the Navy and no longer have a clearance, but it hasn't been that long—our adversaries are not ahead of us in unmanned vehicles, particularly in the autonomy area. I think we have—the robotics center of excellence is in this country, and the marine robotics center of excellence is in this country. And the folks in your district, in Panama City, have leveraged this very highly.

The MK 18 Mod 1 unmanned vehicle, which is based on a REMUS [Remote Environmental Monitoring Units] vehicle which was invented for academic research at Woods Hole by some people from MIT [Massachusetts Institute of Technology], is a classic example of how smart people inside the military leverage commercial technology for a very good purpose. In that case, it was mine hunting.

Mr. CLARK. I think I agree with Admiral Connor on that, that the most capable systems are being developed by American academia, often in consortiums with the U.S. Government.

You see a lot of efforts going on, though, in other countries just to put more and more stuff out there. So the Chinese have a large number of UUVs that they have been developing. The Russians have had a longstanding program that uses unmanned vehicles, and mostly remotely operated vehicles, to go do undersea surveillance or to do work on cables, et cetera. So those programs have been, you know, longstanding efforts by those countries. But they aren't as advanced as the U.S. technologically, but they may try to make up for that in terms of just mass, by putting more effort into it.

The other area where I see, when you look at the technical journals, foreign countries, you know, potentially gaining a level playing field is when it comes to the physics and some of the computer processing power that is available. So how you improve your anti-submarine warfare capabilities involves how do you use the physics of the undersea. Well, that technology is obviously well understood to a lot of people. And so it could be something that academically other countries will leverage and take advantage of the fact that computer processing power has now grown to the point where you can do things today in other countries using their technology that you would only be able to do in the United States in the past.

Ms. GRAHAM. Thank you for that.

As I have spent quite a bit of time at the Naval Support Activity Center in Panama City and I have seen all the incredible things that they are doing—and the private sector. It is not just by coincidence that there is a large growth of companies that are developing undersea technology there, so that they can work together with the Navy. And I think that is an indication of the cooperation between the private and public that we should be encouraging. I am very proud to represent both.

So thank you for that, and I appreciate your answers to the questions.

Mr. Chairman, I yield back.

Mr. FORBES. Mr. Conaway is recognized for 5 minutes.

Mr. CONAWAY. Thank you, Mr. Chairman.

Gentlemen, thanks for being here.

As the Navy considers or looks to the next generation of attack submarines and the capabilities or attributes that will be the key to that, can you talk to me about, is that all manned, or is there a blend between the manned and unmanned platforms that would be appropriate? And what other key attributes should the Navy look at?

Admiral CONNOR. And so, as we look forward, we are looking at manned and unmanned vehicles that go undersea. We tend to call the ones with the people in them "submarines," and we tend to call the unmanned things something else. But, clearly—I think Mr. Clark articulated it very well—there is going to be a synergy in the future between things that are manned and are unmanned.

He referenced the ability of the submarine to be the node for a number of other vehicles undersea. I would add that, in many cases, the submarine might simply be the customer for a number of unmanned devices that are informing them about the environment, whether they are controlled from a submarine or not. They may very well be controlled from shore or from a carrier strike group or an aircraft.

We should get to the point where it doesn't matter because we have been able to network them, and whoever has the best vantage point——

Mr. CONAWAY. Yeah, I have got that part, but what about using them as attack vehicles, armed and dangerous?

Admiral CONNOR. Ah, I see your question. I think the submarine will be the centerpiece of the things that apply lethal force in the undersea. I think we have some not just conceptual work but policy work to do before we have unmanned vehicles that are delivering.

Mr. CONAWAY. The Air Force had that same struggle between air-breathers and others, and today we wouldn't think about not having armed, unmanned—or remotely piloted, excuse me. They are all piloted.

But is there a lesson for the Navy there? Would they get to an answer quicker?

Admiral CONNOR. There are some parallels in that area. The area that is not a parallel is that, when you have an unmanned air vehicle, you have constant communications. You usually have a video feed. There is a person actually in the loop all the time. That degree of precision control is often not available for something operating undersea, and you have to rely on the inherent autonomy of a computer. And the policy issue is, at what point will we let that autonomous computer make a decision to apply lethal force?

Mr. CLARK. Sir, I would say that the major limitation we are going to find pretty soon in autonomy is not so much how smart the computer is on the vehicle but its limited ability to get situational awareness of what is going on around it. So its sensors are going to be imperfect, and so what will happen is——

Mr. CONAWAY. But wouldn't they have the same kind of ability to figure on what is going on around them that the submarine does?

Mr. CLARK. Exactly.

Mr. CONAWAY. Nobody looks outside the portholes in the sub.

Mr. CLARK. Right. No, but what happens is, on the submarine, you have a human who can be accountable for making a decision with uncertain data. So the submarine commander every day makes decisions with a lack of certainty with regard to what is going on around him, and he is accountable for the results of that action. The autonomous vehicle can't be accountable for the actions that it takes in the face of uncertain data.

But what we could see is a situation where unmanned vehicles——

Mr. CONAWAY. But we don't lose unmanned aerial vehicles that don't have a human trigger-puller.

Mr. CLARK. Right. And you could do the same thing undersea.

Mr. CONAWAY [continuing]. Have a trigger-puller either, would you?

Mr. CLARK. Yes, sir. So you could have an undersea system where the unmanned system is in relatively close contact with a submarine, not necessarily continuous coms [communications] but would, you know, be able to relay back to the submarine a situation that it sees, and then the submarine commander or the person on board would make a decision on whether to apply lethal force and be accountable for that decision. But it would require some degree of coordination between the unmanned system and the submarine.

Mr. CONAWAY. Yeah.

And, again, the unmanned systems can be deployed off a submarine or a carrier. How does the Navy not silo up this decision process and take full advantage of these systems—you know, the surface guys between carriers and LCSs [Littoral Combat Ships] and subsurface and all those silo things? How does it avoid not using something to the fullest extent because it was somebody else's idea and we don't like submariners, we like surface guys better?

Admiral CONNOR. Congressman, I think we are past that in many areas. Having managed the ASW fight, which is a team effort between aircraft, surface ships from carrier strike groups, and submarines and fixed systems, we have some fairly highly evolved ways that we can work closely together without fratricide. And there is a fair amount of humility in who does the final act, so to speak.

In fact, this world that we are talking about in undersea that is heavily based on netted systems, in the vast majority of cases, the preferred community to conduct the final attack would probably be the aviators. Because, as we have a wide range of sensors, when we get a contact and we want to quickly turn that contact into disabling the enemy, the platform of choice would probably be a P–8 aircraft.

Mr. CONAWAY. Thank you.

I yield back.

Mr. FORBES. Mr. Johnson is recognized for 5 minutes.

Mr. JOHNSON. Thank you, Mr. Chairman.

Gentlemen, thank you for your testimony today. And thank you for your service to the Nation, as well.

Admiral Connor, how does the Navy intend to incorporate the proliferation of underwater vehicles into existing submarine platforms? And what modifications should the Navy incorporate into future requirements to ensure that they are able to accept a wider range of emerging technologies?

Admiral CONNOR. Congressman, that gets fairly close to the discussion we had with Congressman Courtney in that we have to have the payload capacity and the versatile payload capacity to handle these vehicles.

This year, for the first time in an operational setting, we deployed and retrieved a series of unmanned vehicles doing missions in a place and in a manner that we could not have done with a submarine. However, we did that with a submarine that was equipped with a device we call a dry-deck shelter, which is designed for the deployment and retrieval of Navy SEALs [Sea, Air, Land forces]. And that is a large ocean interface that we carry on the back of the submarines.

As we look to the future, we need to design our submarines such that the vast majority, if not all of them, will have that same ability to deploy and retrieve, and, preferably, we don't have to add some special component that impacts the performance of the submarine in other ways.

So we are learning lessons as we go along. We have made some steps, but those steps are telling us the types of things we need to have so that we can deploy and retrieve in the future.

Mr. JOHNSON. Thank you.

Mr. Clark, do you have anything you would like to add?

Mr. CLARK. Yes, sir.

So the system Admiral Connor is talking about is the Universal Launch and Recovery Module, ULRM. And that system would be really important to be able to launch and recover unmanned vehicles from a submarine more easily without having to have divers and everybody involved.

The other thing we need to do with our submarines, though, is look at how they communicate with the outside world and with the unmanned vehicles they are going to be interfacing with.

Today, you can generally use three ways to communicate from a submarine. One would be the radio frequency spectrum, so that kind of requires that you be above the water in order to use the radio.

The second way is light, so you can use lasers to communicate at relatively short distances. So we would need to equip submarines with ways of using lasers or LEDs [light-emitting diodes] to communicate with unmanned vehicles that are relatively close to them. And that is a pretty high bandwidth communication link, but it is very short-range.

And then acoustic communications, which can actually travel for a very long distance, so hundreds of kilometers, potentially, if you go to low frequencies. Those communications can travel over a very long distance. So we would need to equip submarines with the ability to do those kinds of long-range acoustic communications so that they can form the centerpiece of this battle network in the future.

Mr. JOHNSON. Thank you.

What barriers to innovation must the Navy address to more rapidly field emerging technologies? For the both of you.

Admiral CONNOR. Congressman, I think the two barriers are: funding; and the other one is the willingness to experiment and tolerate failure in addition to success, with the goal of moving forward faster overall.

Mr. CLARK. I think we need to look at how we establish requirements for new programs.

Today, if you are going to start a new acquisition program, you go and develop through a series of years of analysis a set of requirements for that program. That might be acceptable when you are talking about a manned platform that is going to have people on it and is going to be in the force for decades after its introduction.

But for a payload like an unmanned vehicle or a weapon, that may not be the case. There may be a very quick technology refresh cycle on that. So we may be able to have requirements that are less stringent or less comprehensively developed and could be developed in a shorter time. And that would increase the speed with which we could bring these new systems on board.

The other thing I would note is the testing process that we have today can be very cumbersome. A great example of that is the mine warfare mission package for the LCS, which uses a lot of unmanned systems to go look for mines and blow them up. The one problem they are having today is they are finding that some of these unmanned vehicles are not as good as other unmanned vehicles they would prefer to have in the package, but because the test plan doesn't address the fact that you can switch out these unmanned vehicles as you find some that work better than others, they are forced to stick with their original plan and their original, you know, poor-performing vehicle because the test plan doesn't accommodate any changes.

So having more flexibility with regard to testing might be a very important way to encourage, you know, the introduction of new systems that have shown themselves to be more capable than the ones we are currently pursuing.

Mr. JOHNSON. Thank you.

And, with that, I will yield back.

Mr. FORBES. The gentlelady from Missouri, Mrs. Hartzler, is recognized for 5 minutes.

Mrs. HARTZLER. Thank you, Mr. Chairman.

Thank you, gentlemen. This is very interesting. And I had to miss the opening statements, so I apologize if I ask a question you have already covered here.

But, just to be clear, are there any of these, as you call them, unmanned underwater vehicles in operation now, or is this just totally conceptual at this point?

Admiral CONNOR. There are absolutely vehicles operational now.

Mrs. HARTZLER. So how many do we have in our fleet now?

Admiral CONNOR. I don't know the exact number. I would estimate that it is on the order of a couple of hundred if you include in that definition these series of Wave Gliders that we use around the world for oceanographic measurements which we incorporate into how we operate our sonar systems. That is one category.

There are probably upwards of 50 vehicles in use in the mine-countermeasures mission. And that is a mission that has probably been the most proactive in experimenting, and that was because of the urgent need that was developed by the threat of mines in the Strait of Hormuz, which led to an intense program with funding and led to some pretty remarkable results.

Oh, by the way, that program leveraged vehicles that had been put in service by the oceanographic community for some of their needs. So you can see how, when you set the right environment, one organization can quickly build on another organization's success. It is a very collaborative effort.

And then I did mention earlier that we did our first operational deployment and retrieval on a submarine-like mission this year. So it is expanding pretty rapidly.

Mrs. HARTZLER. So there is only one that is actually being launched from the submarine at this point, and that is the one that was used by the Navy SEALs?

Admiral CONNOR. No. There is one variant that is currently deployed by submarines. It is deployed and retrieved by the submarine development squadron that embarks on the submarine.

Mrs. HARTZLER. Okay. Very good.

And I just want to know a little bit more how it works. I want to build on Representative Conaway's point. I have the Predator drone unit in my district, and they do not like to be referred to as unmanned aerial vehicles, which I certainly understand. They are remotely piloted.

So, in this case, are they all remotely controlled? Or you indicated, Mr. Clark, that there may be some option for just a software package where they operate free of human direction. Is that correct?

Mr. CLARK. That is correct. Yes, ma'am. So, today, most of our undersea, underwater, or other unmanned underwater vehicles are automated——

Mrs. HARTZLER. They really are.

Mr. CLARK [continuing]. Or autonomous. Right. They do not have a remote pilot. So a remote pilot diversion would be a remotely operated vehicle [ROV], which is what you might use in the oil and gas industry to go down and do operations at a wellhead. So, for example, the Deepwater Horizon oil spill that we had in the Gulf, we were using ROVs to do a lot of the repair work there to try to close off the spill.

But in the Navy, we use a lot of unmanned undersea vehicles that are truly unmanned, and they use onboard automation in order to go out and conduct their mission. We use them for survey work. For example, the MK 18 Mod 2 was used to look for the Malaysian airliner that went down in the southern Indian Ocean last year.

So they go off, and they can do these survey missions on their own and come back, and the data can be retrieved from them. What we are talking about is expanding the use of those systems now to do other missions than simply surveying, you know, to look at them for weapons, for example, because they can go out and actually attack something if it has been defined, especially like a fixed target that you could define well in advance.

You could also use them to go do ASW operations by dragging a rig behind them and then being able to search for a contact, that kind of stuff.

So we are looking to expand their use into a lot more areas. But they aren't remotely operated; they are truly unmanned.

Mrs. HARTZLER. Now, last question, you talked about the three ways it could be run—through radar, laser, acoustic. I was just wondering, if they are acoustic, does that make them vulnerable to intentional detection?

Mr. CLARK. Right. It does. It depends on how you do it. So there are ways, just like radio communications, to encrypt those communications underwater. There are also ways to make them less detectable by making the beam very focused so it is hard to intercept it from outside a very narrow beam width. And you can also make it so that the sound is not too far above the noise level of the overall ocean, so you would have a difficult time finding it. You know, if you were trying to listen for the communication, it would just barely rise above the background noise.

Mrs. HARTZLER. Very interesting. Thank you.

I yield back.

Mr. FORBES. If the gentlelady would yield, one of the things that might be interesting for any of our members to do is get a classified briefing on some of the unmanned operations that are going out there. I think that would be insightful too.

With that, the gentlelady from Hawaii, Ms. Gabbard, is recognized for 5 minutes.

Ms. GABBARD. Thank you. Thanks, Mr. Chairman.

Thank you, gentlemen, for being here.

And, on that note, I would like to encourage my colleagues to come out and visit the Barking Sands facility in my district, where a lot of this innovative training is taking place in 900 square nautical miles, water depths ranging from 6,000 to 15,000 feet, with a full spectrum of range support and data display, target weapon launching, recovery, et cetera, et cetera. It is something that we are proud of, and it is a one-of-a-kind asset that we have here for our Navy to use.

Mr. Clark, I wonder if you could speak a little bit more to something that you mentioned earlier with regards to transitioning R&D [research and development] technologies from DARPA into acquisition programs. And you mentioned about the need to move away from transitioning directly to warfighters to focusing more for DARPA on kind of these bigger, longer-term innovative ideas.

If you could talk a little bit about the balance of that, given some of the present-day challenges we are facing as well as the projected challenges and increased capabilities we are seeing in other parts of the world.

Mr. CLARK. Yes, ma'am. So our service organizations that do research and development—for example, the Office of Naval Research—are designed to be pursuing near-term advancements to current capabilities. So they would be the organizations that are looking to take existing systems that we have today and adding new capabilities to them through their research projects or introducing some new systems that sort of build upon what the current system of systems that we may have in the DOD does.

So that is more of the evolutionary change. It is going to come from those organizations. What we need DARPA and organizations like that—and this is also where the, you know, kind of, outside-DOD innovation industry could be looking, as well—is, how are we getting ahead to deal with the next set of challenges?

So the near-term challenges are: We have new competitors that are fielding submarines. We have to be able to, you know, detect and potentially engage them. And we have to maintain our ability to gain access undersea in places where people don't want us to go. I mean, those are things we have talked about with unmanned vehicles, et cetera.

But we need to start looking down the road at, what is the next generation of anti-submarine warfare detection technologies? If it is not going to be passive acoustic sonar, is it going to be something else? DARPA should be looking at what is that next game-changing technology.

If we are going to go to vehicles that can do on their own everything that a base submarine would do, then how do we build that autonomy and build that sensor capability—because they go together—into the next generation of vehicles to enable these totally different operating concepts that we might use, where an unmanned vehicle goes and does an operation in place of a submarine?

Those are the things that a DARPA-type organization should be looking at. So they are fairly disruptive. They are pretty revolutionary. They are going to involve some risk. But if nobody is looking at that, then we won't be able to gain that next advantage.

So a good example would be things like stealth. You know, we wouldn't have had stealth if DARPA hadn't started pursuing it 20 years before we ever fielded the first stealth airplane.

Ms. GABBARD. And, on that note, Admiral, at the end of your written testimony, you talked about innovation and incentivizing that innovation, which goes directly along with what you are talking about.

Can you give some examples of how we can best incentivize private investment towards this development and open up the doors more for those who are doing the research and finding solutions for this in the private sector and eliminating some of those obstacles to the DOD being able to take action?

Admiral CONNOR. Yes, ma'am. I would be happy to do that.

I will give you an example. In the field of autonomy, for example, you know, autonomy engines, which are really software algorithms that help machines make decisions independent of operator, it is a very quickly moving field. Most of the development that is taking place there is taking place in the private sector. Much of what they are developing is directly applicable to the type of work that we do in national defense.

If we want to be able to leverage the best types of algorithms that come into our programs, we will need to provide a way, for example, that the rights to that intellectual property when we incorporate it still provide a reward to the person who designed it in a way that makes them want to keep working with us and that makes their competitors want to design something better that we want to buy.

And it is an incredibly fast-moving field. And that is just one example. There are other parallels in propulsion, that the battery industry is moving forward at a very rapid pace, and whoever has the best battery, which has a big impact on the system, should be rewarded for that.

Ms. GABBARD. Thank you.

Thank you, Mr. Chairman.

Mr. FORBES. Mr. Larsen is recognized for 5 minutes.

Mr. LARSEN. Thank you, Mr. Chairman.

So, a little over a year ago, I was out fishing about 20 miles off the coast of Neah Bay with former Congressman Norm Dicks, and there were two things I discovered that weekend: One, I am a better fisherman than Norm Dicks. And that is for the record. That is for the record. It is a pretty high bar. Second, there is a lot of water out there, a lot of water out there. And so that physical limit, if you will, applies to us as much as it applies to peer competitors and near-peer competitors, to cover that water.

So, Admiral Connor or Mr. Clark, can you talk a little bit more about the sheer numbers? If you went to ROVs or autonomous, to cover the kind of water that we would need to cover, you would need a lot, unless you made a conscious decision to, you know, limit the space that you are going to cover at any one time. And so how do you address it? It is sort of the—it is not the tyranny of distance; it is the tyranny of volume.

Admiral CONNOR. Congressman, I would be happy to answer that.

This is a case where you don't have to know everything everywhere, but there are some places where you would like to have very good knowledge. So if you take some of the more strategic chokepoints in the world, the approaches to them, you would want to gain near-perfect knowledge in those areas.

When we have critical things we want to protect, like some of the undersea infrastructure that we mentioned earlier that is so critical to our economy, there may be places where you decide you want to have a volume of system in that relatively small area around that infrastructure where you would have sufficient vehicles for perfect knowledge. And then you would need, obviously, a different approach to, you know, open ocean.

The other area where we want to have fairly perfect knowledge is the area around things like our carrier strike groups. And all of the examples that I mentioned are doable if we take that system-of-systems approach, recognizing that some systems are suited to, say, a deepwater environment and others are more suitable for a chokepoint environment.

And the task that the Navy has to come up with is how to combine varying systems in a way that they present an output that is easy to understand by the operators so that they don't have to worry so much about the physics of shallow versus deep water; they just have to know where the contact is. And that is doable if we just apply some operational planning and decide what areas are important.

Mr. LARSEN. Uh-huh.

Mr. CLARK. So one thing I would add to that—I think that is exactly right when it comes to areas that we are trying to defend. I think, then, looking for the adversary's problem, we want to force the same problem onto him. So we don't need to have a large number of underseas systems in his near-abroad to force him now into a situation where he is expending a lot of effort to go find where we are. So the combination of submarines with unmanned systems would enable us to be able to distribute our force over enough area that it creates fits for him in terms of his anti-submarine warfare efforts.

The other thing it points out is the urgent need for the DOD to develop counter-UUV technologies. Because finding an unmanned underwater vehicle is very hard because they are small, they are usually made of plastic, they don't have a great sonar return. So developing ways to counter the efforts of others to bring UUVs against us is very important, because that could be one of the asymmetric capabilities of the future, like we saw with the IEDs [improvised explosive devices] and now we are seeing UAVs. UUVs may be another capability somebody could use against us asymmetrically.

Mr. LARSEN. Yeah.

I want to follow up on something Mr. Wittman and Ms. Gabbard discussed, but I am still not hearing the specifics, and this is how to get private sector to participate more in this particular area, especially as it relates to IP [intellectual property].

I forget which one of you mentioned it in your testimony more specifically, but there is a problem with who gets to keep that intellectual property and who has to sign it over. It is usually the Navy gets to keep it, and the private sector has to sign it over. That is not going to work long term if we want the private sector to participate.

Can you talk a little bit more about how you could make that work?

Admiral CONNOR. One way to make that work is to start buying stuff. I know it sounds pretty simple, but when defense contractors would come to me, they would look at our budget and they would look at the size of the budget and they would look at the probability that they could gain that business, and then they would make a decision as to how to invest their own money.

And so, if we recognize that this is a growing field and we make a conscious attempt to lead-turn this dynamic field by investing in the technology that is coming to bear in a short period of time, that will snowball and others will join the business, and our capacity will get greater, but also the quality of the systems will get greater because American entrepreneurs will make an attempt to gain our business.

Mr. CLARK. The other thing I would say is we could look at leasing more systems. As unmanned underwater vehicles become more common, both commercially and in the military, we could lease more of these systems.

And that is a similar model to what we have used the UAVs, so the ScanEagle and some of the other UAVs that we have used off Navy ships. In many cases, most of them we have today have been leased, and it is contractor-owned/contractor-operated, and we just rent the thing.

So those are options that are going to present themselves to us as unmanned underwater vehicles become more common.

Mr. LARSEN. Thank you.

Mr. FORBES. Gentlemen, thank you very much.

As we mentioned at the outset, we always like to give our witnesses a few moments. If there is anything that you didn't get a chance to elaborate on as much as you thought you should have or if there were any questions that you would like to clarify an answer on, this would be the time to do that.

And, Admiral, why don't we once again start with you, and we will let Mr. Clark have the final word.

Admiral CONNOR. Chairman Forbes, thank you again for letting us talk to you today.

The points that I would like to just add that I didn't mention earlier is that one of the areas we didn't talk about very much was the risk that adversary systems might present to our infrastructure and the urgency with which we should seek to come up with efficient ways to defend our infrastructure—oil and gas, coms, power, et cetera. And that should be a consideration. And that mission will probably fall to the Navy if it is greater than 12 miles from land.

And then, lastly, we talked about developments in laser coms and autonomy and so forth, and I just want to thank you all, because we had made some great strides in very recent time simply with the funding that was allocated to those efforts via the omnibus reprogramming earlier this year. And all the committees that made that happen had a direct impact in pushing forward a dynamic field in a very big way. I was at Woods Hole yesterday, and they were showing me all the great work that they did with the money you provided only a few months ago.

Thank you.

Mr. FORBES. Good. Thank you.

Mr. Clark.

Mr. CLARK. Thank you, sir. Thank you again for having us here today. It has been a terrific experience and honor.

I would have two things that I wanted to add. We talked a little bit earlier about diesel submarines. Congressman Wittman brought them up. One thing I would say with regard to diesel submarines, our experience with World War II diesel submarine warfare, which is the largest scale of anti-submarine warfare competition that we have had, was that diesel submarines could be rendered ineffective by mounting a pretty aggressive anti-submarine warfare campaign even if you didn't sink any submarines.

The Germans, the Italians, even the Americans, when faced with somebody that was aggressively going after them with active sonar and even ineffective attacks, were successful at keeping the diesel submarines from being able to operate and do counter-shipping attacks.

So diesel submarines, while they are cheaper, probably, and maybe could be bought in larger numbers, also suffer from some disadvantages that would make them easier to prevent from being effective because they are slow and they lack the ability to endure underwater for a very long time.

The second point I would bring up is on this point of innovation and organization, is that the Navy's recent effort to align all of its unmanned systems under a single directorate I think offers some opportunities to improve the speed with which and the effectiveness with which it can transition new capabilities. So I would applaud that.

I think we have to take a similar approach in the acquisition world, to look for ways to align under one organization these smaller programs that lead to technological advancements. Because today they are often under a larger organization that has much bigger responsibilities for large acquisition programs that are going to consume all of their time and consume most of their money.

So they don't have the brainpower and the bandwidth to be able to look closely at the technology efforts and see which ones are offering the most promise and foster those and then, you know, take the other ones and take them off the plate and cancel them. And so one of the reasons we see today that we have a lot of programs bubbling up but very few get turned off is because the people that manage those programs don't have the time to devote to be able to determine which ones to keep and which ones to get rid of.

So I think that is a good effort on the requirements side that the OPNAV [Office of the Chief of Naval Operations] staff is taking. We need to follow suit within our acquisition organizations in the Navy to be able to carry that through so that unmanned systems and the innovative technologies they incorporate can be, you know, taken forward in a strategic way as opposed to simply in a bottoms-up, water-all-the-flowers approach like we have now.

Mr. FORBES. Could you just take a couple seconds and clarify on the diesel subs, since it has been raised? The admiral mentioned they could go about 100 miles and then they had to come up to the surface. Can you explain why, so we have that on the record?

Mr. CLARK. Right. So a diesel sub is going to be able to operate on its battery and use battery to drive an electric motor to go around underwater, but that battery will eventually need to be recharged. And so the diesel engine is then operated to recharge the battery, which means you have to come up and put the snorkel up in order to get air to run the diesel.

Even air-independent propulsion submarines, which use an engine that uses a chemical oxidant instead of air to be able to run a diesel engine and recharge the battery, have a limited amount of that chemical oxidant on board. So, after a couple of weeks, they have to go and replace their chemical oxidant, so they are pretty limited in their endurance, as well.

So non-nuclear submarines offer some opportunities, but they have significant limitations when it comes to how long they can stay underwater.

Mr. FORBES. Admiral.

Admiral CONNOR. If I could just clarify, if I implied that a diesel submarine could only go 100 miles without a recharge, that is not what I meant to convey. What I meant is——

Mr. FORBES. Maybe I misunderstood. You said about 100 miles in a day, I think.

Admiral CONNOR. Right. And then they have to recharge, depending on how their technology is, every 2 to 5 days. But when you work against them, on average, you know they are not going to make much more than that, or if they are, they are going to make noise.

Mr. FORBES. Okay.

Well, thank you both for being with us.

And if there are no other questions, then we are adjourned.

[Whereupon, at 4:03 p.m., the subcommittee was adjourned.]

APPENDIX

OCTOBER 27, 2015

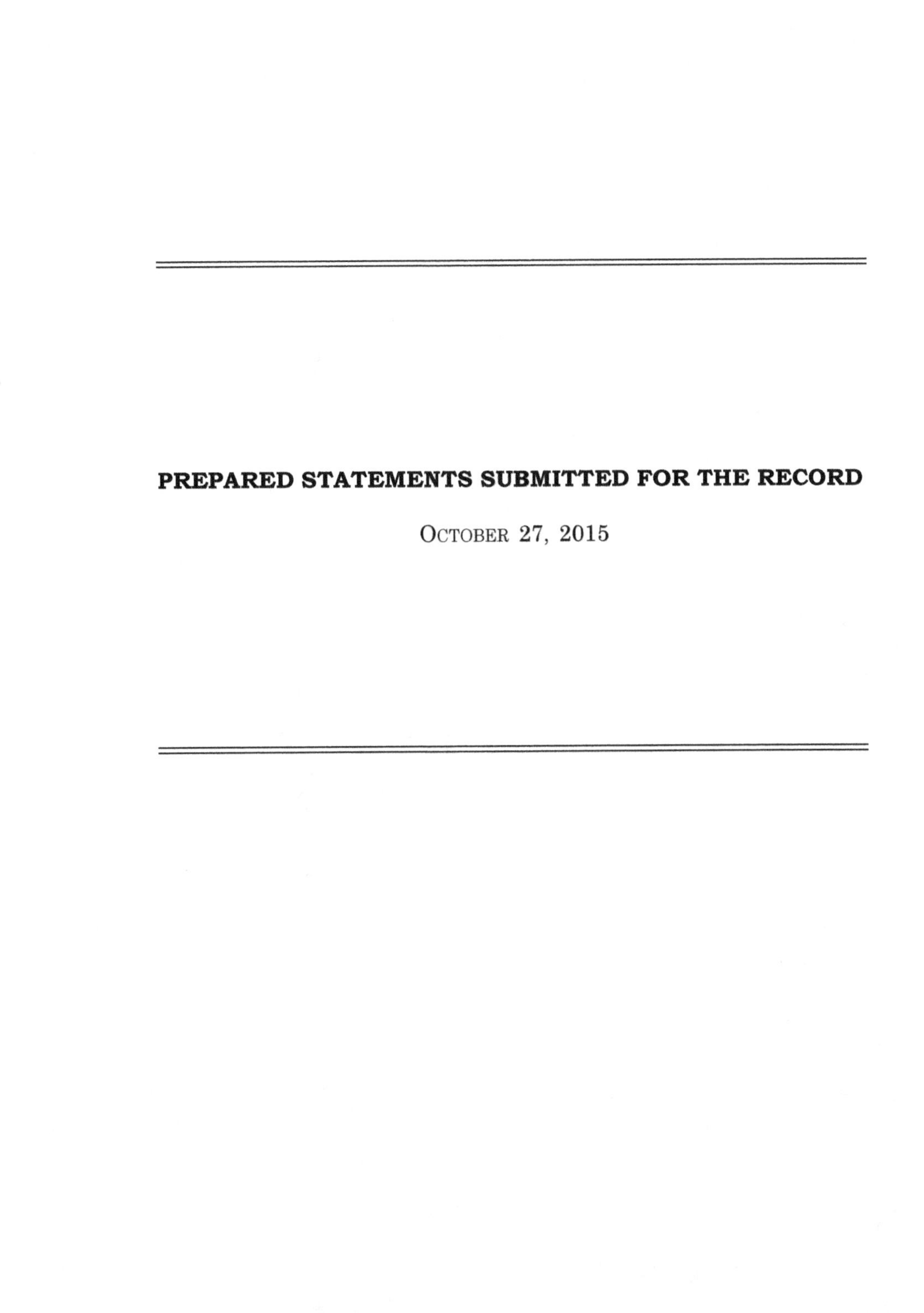

PREPARED STATEMENTS SUBMITTED FOR THE RECORD

OCTOBER 27, 2015

**Opening Remarks of the Honorable J. Randy Forbes
for the
Seapower and Projection Forces Hearing on
Game Changers—Undersea Warfare
October 27, 2015**

As the members of this Subcommittee and our witnesses are well aware, America's ability to project power overseas is currently being challenged by the rapid growth of other nations' military forces and the fielding of novel capabilities that undermine our freedom of maneuver and action and threaten to deprive our nation of the many benefits we derive from our command of the seas. If we remain on our present trajectory, I fear we may see our seapower and power projection capabilities eclipsed, and our influence eroded in critical regions overseas.

In the past, Congress has responded to similar threats by undertaking great expansions of our air and maritime forces. Championed by legislators like Carl Vinson, these buildups reenergized American seapower and projection forces and sustained them for another generation.

Given the challenges and constraints we face today, however, I believe a different response from Congress and the Pentagon is required. Building <u>more</u> things will be part of the solution, but it is my belief that what we really need at present are <u>new</u> things—innovative capabilities and concepts that will "change the game" in the many areas of military competition where the trends are unfavorable.

Today, this Subcommittee kicks off a series of hearings examining potentially "game-changing" concepts and capabilities with a look at the undersea domain. This is a domain in which the United States has for decades been dominant—and benefited immensely from it. Our superiority in this domain has enabled the United States to surreptitiously collect sensitive intelligence, hold at risk foreign fleets, attack targets on land without warning, and maintain the secure second-strike capability that is essential for deterrence.

While surface ships and forces ashore are coming under increased threat from anti-access/area-denial capabilities and being forced to operate at longer ranges, U.S. submarines still enjoy freedom of maneuver and the ability to operate with near impunity under the sea. In the view of many respected defense leaders and analysts, this provides an enduring strategic advantage that the United States should leverage to "offset" competitors' growing strength in other areas.

Unfortunately, as with so many elements of our fleet, the demand for undersea forces currently exceeds the supply—and the situation is forecast to grow worse. At present, the U.S. submarine fleet is able to meet only 65% of commanders' requests for forces. Under current plans, the Navy's submarine fleet will shrink by 25% between now and 2030, with our fleet of attack submarines shrinking from 53 to 41 boats. Over that same time period, we stand to lose 60% of our undersea payload capacity as our four SSGNs are retired from service.

So, at a time when our submarine force will likely be called upon to do more than ever, it is also going to be at its smallest size since World War II. At the same time, our existing sensors and weapons should be expected to decline in effectiveness as our adversaries' own capabilities improve.

Fortunately, the submarine community is aware of the challenges and opportunities it faces, and we are privileged to have two of its leading thinkers here before us to discuss them:

- Retired Vice Admiral Michael J. Connor, Former Commander, Submarine Forces;
- Mr. Bryan Clark, Senior Fellow at the Center for Strategic and Budgetary Assessments.

These two submariners have been at the forefront of undersea innovation, and I am eager to hear from them what new undersea concepts and capabilities the Navy is currently developing, and what more might be done to sustain and exploit our dominance in that critically important domain.

Opening Remarks for Congressman Joe Courtney
Ranking Member
Seapower and Projection Forces Subcommittee
Game Changers – Undersea Warfare
October 27, 2015

Mr. Chairman, thank you for calling today's hearing on "game changers" in undersea warfare, capabilities and technologies.

Our undersea capabilities remains one of the most distinctive and asymmetrical advantages for our nation. One of the greatest challenges we face, however, is the rapid developments in undersea sensors, capabilities and platforms around the world. The reality is that this significant and hard-earned edge in the undersea realm is perishable if we do not do all we can now to maintain this core advantage for the future.

The pressure that our submarine force faces in the coming decade is well known. While the current Block IV multi-year contract sustains the two-a-year build rate through 2018, the Navy's 30 year shipbuilding plan for fiscal year 2016 includes several years where that rate slows to one a year starting in 2021, the first year of the Ohio Replacement Program. The plan shows a 16 year period between 2025 and 2041 when the attack submarine force structure falls below minimum levels needed to meet the requirement.

Given that the submarine force today is only able to fill just over half the requests for submarine presence by our combatant commanders, this looming shortfall will force the Submarine Force, and our nation, to do more under the sea with fewer platforms. This will require us to look at different ways to deploy and utilize our submarines and become more innovative in using advanced technologies to maximize the reach, capabilities and effectiveness of a reduced fleet.

Key to the future capabilities of our submarine force is the Virginia Payload Module. This 90-foot insert into Virginia-class submarines to be built in Block V and later will help mitigate the 60 percent reduction in undersea strike capabilities that will be lost when the current fleet of four SSGNs retires in the next decade. As important, VPM must also be a flexible and versatile platform to support unmanned underwater vehicles and a wide range of potential innovations to expand the reach of our undersea force through integration of non-strike payloads.

Of particular bipartisan concern for this subcommittee is the current plan for incorporating VPM into future submarines. While the requirement for this program calls for 20 VPM-enabled submarines, the current budget projection only plans for the inclusion of VPM into just one submarine a year starting in 2019. Adding the module in at a rate of one a year is simply not a pace that can match the loss of undersea strike and payload deployment capabilities we lose with the retirement of the four SSGNs. I look forward to continuing to work with Chairman Forbes and our colleagues to closely examine the Navy's plan to incorporate VPM into our submarine fleet.

Beyond the core platforms of the Virginia class, Virginia Payload Module, and the Ohio Replacement, it is important to also focus the constellation of capabilities that will form the core of our nation's continued edge in the undersea realm. With reduced numbers of attack submarines and SSGNs available in the next decade, it is critical that our navy retains access to a broad range of autonomous sensors, unmanned vehicles and other technologies during this period to fill the gap and expand the reach of our submarines.

We are privileged to have with us today Admiral Mike Connor, who recently retired from his career in the Navy after serving as Commander Submarine Forces. Under his leadership, the Submarine Force developed the Undersea Dominance Campaign Plan to articulate a vision of what our undersea capabilities should look like in 2025. The challenge for Congress, the Navy and industry is to turn this vision of undersea warfare a decade from now into concrete investments and tangible capabilities in the field. From conception to funding, testing and fielding, we must work together to turn this vision for continued undersea dominance into reality.

Innovation is in the blood of the submarine force and the industrial base that supports it. With the right leadership and support, we can harness this legacy of innovation to retain and expand our undersea edge. I look forward to the testimony of our two distinguished witnesses to provide insight to this subcommittee as to the importance of current efforts underway today, challenges that must be overcome, and game changing areas that this panel and the Navy should be focused on moving ahead.

Testimony of Vice Admiral (retired) Michael J. Connor

before the

United States House of Representatives Armed Services Committee

Sea Power and Projection Forces Committee Hearing

Game Changers – Undersea Warfare

October 27, 2015

Chairman Forbes, Ranking Member Courtney, members and staff, thank you for the invitation to speak here today on the topic of game changers in undersea warfare. I also want to thank all of you on this committee for the support that you provided to the Submarine Force during my tenure as commander for three years from 2012 to 2015. The long term commitments that you made to the shipbuilding program created the foundation for the consistent superior performance of the Virginia class program which continues to deliver submarines ahead of schedule and under budget.

That type of support will continue to be important going forward because dominance in the undersea domain will be even more important in the future than it has been in the past. In today's world, control of the undersea is a necessary prerequisite to sea control and joint force access in the maritime arena. Therefore it underpins commerce, protection of natural resources and homeland defense.

The undersea arena is the most opaque of all warfighting domains. It is easier to track a small object in space than it is to track a large submarine, with tremendous fire power under the water. That is why countries with the technical wherewithal to operate in this domain are pursuing advanced capability. The two countries that present the biggest challenge in the undersea are Russian and China, with Russia being the more capable of the two.

With both Russia and China pursuing territorial expansion at the same time they are delivering much improved submarines with more advanced weapon systems, now is a good time to sustain our advantage in the undersea, and leverage that advantage with game-changing capabilities. This hearing topic shows that this committee understands this. Therefore I would like to continue with some recommendations as how this committee can help deliver those game-changing capabilities.

You will be happy to know that the Navy has a strategy to guide their way ahead in the undersea. I briefed some of you on that strategy earlier this year in a classified setting.

First, we need to continue our commitment to having the best submarines. The side with the quietest submarines with the best sensors has both tangible and intangible advantages. The tangible advantage is simple the ability to strike your foe at a greater range than he can strike you. The intangible advantage is even greater. An adversary that never really knows if there is a submarine in the area, and capable of striking on short notice, can never have confidence that they can control the sea. Many of you know from your closed hearings that we have significant advantage with our submarines against potential foes. The question for today however, comes down to whether we are fully leveraging that advantage with the right type of payloads to achieve a full effect.

The first step we need to take, and are taking, is to extend the striking range of our submarine-launched weapons. This multiplies the impact of each submarine and multiplies the search challenge that each submarine presents to a potential foe. In the case of torpedoes, we should be pursuing a design objective of an effective range in excess of 100 miles. This is definitely doable with chemical-based propulsion systems and will likely soon be achievable with battery systems. To effectively leverage this range, we need enhanced command and control systems, including the ability to communicate with a torpedo at a range of 100 miles. It is very likely that in the future the final instructions for a submarine launched torpedo will come via manned or unmanned aircraft, or via satellite. The torpedo will come to be considered along the line of a slow moving missile, with the advantage that it is more difficult to detect, carries a much larger explosive charge, and strikes the enemy beneath the waterline, where the impact is most severe.

The next step we need to take is to get back into the business of submarine-launched anti-ship missiles. We abandoned that capability about 20 years ago because we had difficulty with the technology of the day ensuring that the missile would hit only the desired target. Command and control technology has improved a lot since then. US industry has today, the ability to build an anti-ship missile that can be launched from a submarine (or a surface ship) and confidently attack a specific target at sea at a range of about 1000 miles. We should be pursuing this more aggressively than we are. The impact would be enormous. While the destructive force of a missile is far less than that of a torpedo, a missile will often render the adversary combat ineffective. Further, when you combine a stealthy submarine with a long-range missile, you put the adversary in the position of having to maintain an air-defense posture whenever there is a possibility that a US submarine might be within missile range. That requires the enemy to replace many of his offensive weapons with defensive weapons. It requires him to operate air defense radar systems, making him easy to detect. It also requires him to aggressively respond to the slightest indication that there may be a submarine in the area. In other words, extending the striking range of a US submarine is a cost-imposing, asymmetric improvement. I would note that many of those same advantages accrue to a surface ship employing a long range weapon. That is why the surface force and the submarine force are working together to close that gap.

Next, we need to expand the rate at which the force gathers information to inform both strategic and tactical decisions. It needs to be done at greater ranges and in multiple locations. This will be the job of unmanned vehicles—in the air, on the sea and under the sea. As you know, the submarine force achieved an important milestone this year with the operational deployment and recovery of unmanned vehicles doing a series of missions that would have been either impossible or untenable from a risk perspective. That was in important milestone, but it was only the first of many milestones that must be achieved. Going forward, we need to improve the endurance of the vehicles, expand the payload set, and get to the point where any submarine can recover the mission data, if not the vehicle. We need to do this while keeping the cost of the vehicle down. The cost should be low enough such that, while we would always like to get the vehicles back, it is not a crisis if we don't. The value is in the data, not the vehicle.

Unmanned vehicles that produce game-changing effects in the undersea domain include many vehicles that would be deployed by other means than submarines. The key is that we need to expand the number of sensors we can place in the field, and develop the means of harvesting the output of those sensors. To the extent that we succeed in this area, we make each of our capital assets--our submarines, ships, and aircraft-- that much more effective. This will be a system of systems approach. The particular systems that we should use will vary as a function of the environment and the mission. For example, some systems are well suited to deep water and others to shallow water. We will need to build the systems and then create an easy to understand output for the fleet commanders that is common to all sensors. In fact, the information architecture that displays the output of undersea systems would ideally be common with those hosting the output of any other surveillance and reconnaissance system. We don't operate this way today, but we should in the future. If we do this right, we will keep our expensive and over-tasked ships, submarines and aircraft focused on doing the types of things that only they can do or should do. We should to a large degree turn over the role of search to unmanned systems. The opportunity space here is huge for both government and industry. Next, I would like to talk to you about how you can help the Department of Defense, and the defense industrial base make that happen.

There are a number of game-changing programs that are under way. They were funded, in part, on the omnibus reprogramming earlier this year. We appreciate the efforts of the authorizers and appropriators in the House and Senate that made that happen. That effort greatly expands our use of groundbreaking unmanned sensors to solve near term problems. It has unleashed a wave of energy and creativity in the system development community. That effort will be fielded in 2016 and key milestones along the way to fielding are being met.

That brings me to the larger picture of how the Department of Defense and the Congress can work together to develop undersea technology at a pace that keeps us ahead of peer competitors and allows progress at the rate that American technologists can produce it. Game changing breakthroughs will not be permanent solutions. Rather, they will be a competitive advantage that will last for a finite period of time. The future will require an innovation cycle that produces game changing solutions again and again.

The Federal Budget Process is slow and time consuming. I don't need to remind you of that—especially this week. The Department of Defense will spend a year developing a budget for submission to the Congress. It is typically delivered in February. Congress spends 6-9 months approving and modifying it for submission to the President, with no guarantee that it will not be vetoed. Sometimes we have short term continuing resolutions to keep basic functions operating, although no new starts or innovation projects are permitted to begin during the duration of the continuing resolution.

The issue is that we need a method to keep the pace of innovation alive in a world in which the technology cycle is only 2-3 years. If we work each new idea and proposed program via a specific new proposed line item in the budget, each new game-changing initiative will consume an entire technology cycle awaiting budget approval. In a world in which the pace of technology is fast and getting faster, one of our crucial strategic advantages will have to be the ability to innovate faster than our adversaries.

Help from Congress in sustaining rapid innovation despite the realities of the federal budget process requires the following steps:

First, Congress should provide innovation funding that is not tied to specific programs of record.

Second, programs should be defined broadly so that they can incorporate innovation without recreating the program. This process is already working well in the submarine combat system area, but needs to be incorporated in the torpedo area as we begin a much overdue heavyweight torpedo production restart.

Third, we should have the ability to recognize failure when we see it and cut our losses. If we are innovating aggressively enough, perhaps half of our initiatives will fail. We should embrace that failure, cut funding to the program, and apply that funding in other endeavors. Of note, in the most innovative area on the planet, Silicon Valley, that failure rate approaches 90%. You see failure often, usually when a program manager comes to you with a proposal for 'restructuring.' Sometimes a request for restructuring really means that the underlying technology or operating concept did not work. When that is the case, it is time to learn the lessons and move on.

Fourth, if we are to truly harness the innovation of this country, without breaking the bank in innovation research, we need to ensure that we provide a means for companies in the private sector to keep control of their intellectual property and harvest the profits when we find their innovations useful. That provides the incentive for private investment, which tends to be much more efficient than government innovation investment. There has never been a better time than now, as much of the technology that was developed in the energy, communications, and academic research sectors can be applied to the defense sector with minor modifications.

Once again, I would like to thank you for the opportunity to speak here today and I wish you well as you endeavor to support game changing innovation in the undersea arena. I would be happy to answer any of your questions.

Vice Admiral (Retired) Michael J. Connor

A native of Weymouth, Massachusetts, Vice Adm. Michael Connor graduated from Bowdoin College in 1980. He is a Mahan Scholar and distinguished graduate of the Naval War College with a Master of Arts in National Security Affairs and Strategic Studies.

Following completion of his initial nuclear power and submarine training, he served on USS Ulysses S. Grant (SSBN 631), USS Pittsburgh (SSN 720), USS Providence (SSN 719), and USS Augusta (SSN 710).

Connor commanded USS Seawolf (SSN 21) from 1997 to 2000. He served as commander, Submarine Squadron 8 from March 2003 through July 2004. From June 2008 until April 2010, he served as commander, Submarine Group 7, Task Force 54/74 Yokosuka, Japan.

Connor's shore assignments include service at the Navy Operational Intelligence Center; flag secretary for the Commander, Submarine Force, U.S. Atlantic Fleet; prospective commanding officer instructor for U.S. Atlantic Fleet. He has served on the Joint Staff, on the staff of the Assistant Secretary of the Navy; as director, Submarine Warfare Division (N87); director, Naval Warfare Integration Group (N00X); and, assistant deputy chief of Naval Operations for Warfare Systems (N9B) on the OPNAV staff. He served as commander, Submarine Forces from September 2012 until September 2015.

His personal awards include the Distinguished Service Medal (two awards), Defense Superior Service Medal, Legion of Merit (four awards), Meritorious Service Medal (three awards), Navy and Marine Corps Commendation Medal (three awards), and Navy and Marine Corps Achievement Medal (two awards).

DISCLOSURE FORM FOR WITNESSES
COMMITTEE ON ARMED SERVICES
U.S. HOUSE OF REPRESENTATIVES

INSTRUCTION TO WITNESSES: Rule 11, clause 2(g)(5), of the Rules of the U.S. House of Representatives for the 114th Congress requires nongovernmental witnesses appearing before House committees to include in their written statements a curriculum vitae and a disclosure of the amount and source of any federal contracts or grants (including subcontracts and subgrants), or contracts or payments originating with a foreign government, received during the current and two previous calendar years either by the witness or by an entity represented by the witness and related to the subject matter of the hearing. This form is intended to assist witnesses appearing before the House Committee on Armed Services in complying with the House rule. Please note that a copy of these statements, with appropriate redactions to protect the witness's personal privacy (including home address and phone number) will be made publicly available in electronic form not later than one day after the witness's appearance before the committee. Witnesses may list additional grants, contracts, or payments on additional sheets, if necessary.

Witness name: _Michael J. Connor_

Capacity in which appearing: (check one)

◉ Individual

◯ Representative

If appearing in a representative capacity, name of the company, association or other entity being represented: _N/A_

Federal Contract or Grant Information: If you or the entity you represent before the Committee on Armed Services has contracts (including subcontracts) or grants (including subgrants) with the federal government, please provide the following information:

2015

Federal grant/contract	Federal agency	Dollar value	Subject of contract or grant
None			

2014

Federal grant/ contract	Federal agency	Dollar value	Subject of contract or grant
none			

2013

Federal grant/ contract	Federal agency	Dollar value	Subject of contract or grant
none			

<u>Foreign Government Contract or Payment Information</u>: If you or the entity you represent before the Committee on Armed Services has contracts or payments originating from a foreign government, please provide the following information:

2015

Foreign contract/ payment	Foreign government	Dollar value	Subject of contract or payment
none			

2014

Foreign contract/ payment	Foreign government	Dollar value	Subject of contract or payment
none			

2013

Foreign contract/ payment	Foreign government	Dollar value	Subject of contract or payment
none			

**STATEMENT BEFORE THE HOUSE ARMED SERVICES SEAPOWER AND
PROJECTION FORCES SUBCOMMITTEE ON
"GAME CHANGERS – UNDERSEA WARFARE"**

October 27, 2015

**Statement by Bryan Clark
Senior Fellow, Center for Strategic and Budgetary Assessments**

Today the U.S. Navy is dominant in undersea warfare. Its quiet submarines can operate with near-impunity throughout the world's oceans and most littoral waters. Its long-range surveillance systems are able to monitor many of the strategically or economically important maritime crossroads. And its anti-submarine warfare capabilities surpass those of competing militaries in lethality and capacity. As a result, today's U.S. defense strategy depends in large part on America's undersea advantage. Multiple Quadrennial Defense Reviews, National Military Strategies, and Congressional hearing statements highlight how quiet submarines, in particular, are one of the American military's most viable means of gathering intelligence and projecting power in the face of mounting anti-access and area denial (A2/AD) threats being fielded by a growing number of countries.

But America's undersea dominance is not assured—or permanent. U.S. submarines are the world's quietest, but new detection techniques are emerging that don't rely on the noise a submarine generates and may make some traditional manned submarine operations riskier in the future. America's competitors are likely pursuing these technologies even while growing and quieting their own undersea forces. To affordably sustain its undersea advantage well into this century, the U.S. Navy must accelerate innovation in undersea warfare by evolving the role of manned submarines and exploiting emerging technologies to field a new "family of undersea systems."

How America came to dominate the undersea

The U.S. Navy did not always "own" the undersea domain. It was an early adopter of submarine technology, but American boats were fewer and less capable than European countries until the middle of World War II. By that point, the U.S. Navy had grown a relatively large force of ocean-going U.S. submarines to sustain a successful counter-shipping campaign against the Japanese. Except for Germany and Russia, European submarine fleets had shrunk due to disrepair, combat losses, and capture. In the aftermath of World War II, the Soviet Navy

1667 K Street, NW, Suite 900, Washington, DC 20006   Tel.202-331-7990
www.CSBAonline.org   Fax.202-331-8019

had the world's largest submarine force, owing to its own construction program and that it gained control of about half the German fleet following its surrender.

With the addition of Germany's fleet, the Soviets also took possession of the most advanced submarines then in production. For example, the German Type XXI U-boat incorporated a snorkel to enable continuous submerged operation, as well as burst communications and X-band radar warning receivers (RWR) to reduce its vulnerability to detection by radar or signals exploitation. This caused great concern in the United States as leaders in and outside the Navy assessed the Soviets could reverse-engineer German submarines and produce them in large numbers to threaten U.S. and allied shipping or the U.S. homeland.

The U.S. Navy pursued ASW capabilities based on active and passive sonar to address the potential Soviet threat. Active sonar showed promise, but passive sonar was not initially effective against diesel submarines because snorkeling submarines sounded like diesel-powered surface ships, and submarines running on battery gave off very little radiated noise.

The U.S. Navy found passive sonar was much more effective against nuclear submarines. In initial exercises against the new USS Nautilus, ASW forces determined they could track the submarine by listening for the pumps and turbines that run continuously in its propulsion plant. Recognizing this potential vulnerability, the U.S. Navy started a methodical sound-silencing program for its nuclear submarines. When the Soviet Navy began fielding nuclear submarines, the American Navy exploited its "first mover" advantage in passive sonar to establish the passive Sound Surveillance System (SOSUS) network off the U.S. coast and at key chokepoints between the Soviet Union and the open ocean.

The combination of passive sonar ASW systems and its own sound-silencing efforts gave the U.S. Navy a significant advantage over relatively noisy Soviet submarines. This overmatch, however, slowly began to erode in the mid-1970s after the Soviet Union learned of their submarines' acoustic vulnerability from the John Walker-led spy ring and obtained technology for submarine quieting from a variety of sources. Newer Soviet submarines such as the *Akula* and *Sierra* classes were much quieter than their predecessors, but were only fielded in small numbers before the Soviet economy began to falter, leading to delayed construction and inadequate sustainment.

In preparation for a time when more quiet submarines were in opposing fleets, the U.S. Navy began exploring other ASW technologies that did not depend on the sound a submarine makes, including new forms of active sonar and non-acoustic methods of detection. These efforts yielded some effective capabilities, such as low-frequency (less than 1000 hertz) active sonar, which was eventually installed on U.S. Navy Surveillance Towed Array Sensor System (SURTASS) ships along with their existing passive sonar arrays.

The urgency behind America's pursuit of new ASW technologies dissipated with the demise of the Soviet Union. Soviet submarine construction and overseas deployments largely stopped, and their advancements in submarine technology did not make their way into other navies. The U.S. Navy was left with undisputed superiority in the undersea domain.

Undersea game changers

Today, new competitors are rising to challenge America's undersea advantage. A resurgent Russia resumed overseas deployments of quiet submarines, a rising and revisionist China is fielding a growing fleet of conventional and nuclear submarines, and competitors including Iran and North Korea are expanding the use of mini-subs in their littorals. At the same time technological advancements, many of them driven by rapid increases in computer processing power or "big data," are empowering new undersea capabilities. Importantly, these new technologies are available to the U.S. military as well.

ASW capabilities. Efforts to protect submarines from being detected since the Cold War have emphasized quieting, since passive sonar is the predominant sensor used for ASW. But today a growing number of new ASW systems do not listen for a submarine's radiated noise. For example, low-frequency active sonar is now widely used by European and Asian navies in variable depth sonar (VDS) systems and will be part of the U.S. Littoral Combat Ship (LCS) ASW mission package. Non-acoustic ASW technologies that detect chemical or radiological emissions or bounce laser light off a submarine are becoming more operationally useful due to improved computer processing and modeling of the undersea environment.

These active sonar and non-acoustic capabilities are likely to be best exploited by mobile platforms such as unmanned vehicles, aircraft, and ships because they are smaller than passive sonar systems. In contrast, to achieve long detection ranges passive sonars must be physically large so they can hear faint noise at the lower frequencies that suffer less attenuation. This makes fixed systems on the sea floor like SOSUS or towed systems such as SURTASS better able to exploit passive sonar improvements.

New ASW technologies, however, will not likely make the ocean transparent or dramatically increase the threat to American submarines in the next one to two decades. Turning a possible submarine detection into a successful ASW engagement involves sifting through a large number of possible submarine detections to find an actual target and then precisely placing an effective weapon on it. What new ASW capabilities could do is increase the chance an American submarine is detected and attacked (albeit ineffectively) in coastal areas where adversary ASW systems are concentrated. Meanwhile, U.S. undersea forces can take actions to defeat enemy ASW capabilities and reduce their vulnerability.

Platform enhancements. The same advancements that are improving ASW capabilities will also enable a new generation of sophisticated counter-detection technologies and techniques. For example, against passive sonar a submarine or unmanned undersea vehicle (UUV) could emit sound to reduce its radiated noise using a technique similar to that of noise cancelling headphones. Against active sonars, undersea platforms could—by themselves or in concert with UUVs and other stationary or floating systems—conduct acoustic jamming or decoy operations similar to those done by electronic warfare systems against radar.

New power and control technologies are improving the endurance and reliability of UUVs, which will likely be able to operate unrefueled for months within the next decade. The autonomy of UUVs will remain constrained, however, by imperfect situational awareness. For example, while a UUV may have the computer algorithms and control systems to avoid safety hazards or security threats, it may not be able to understand with certainty where hazards and threats are and what they are doing. In the face of uncertain data, a human operator can make choices and be accountable for the results. Commanders may not want to place the same responsibility in the hands of a UUV control system—or its programmer.

As sensors and processing improve, UUVs will progressively gain more autonomy in operating safely and securely while accomplishing their missions. In the meantime, the U.S. Navy can expect to shift some operations to unmanned systems for which the consequences of an incorrect decision are limited to damage and loss of the vehicle, rather than loss of life or unplanned military escalation. These missions could include deploying payloads such as sensors or inactive mines, conducting surveillance or surveys, or launching UAVs for electronic warfare. For missions where a human decision-maker is needed, unmanned systems can operate in concert with submarines or use radio communications to regularly "check-in" with commanders.

Undersea payloads. The ability of undersea platforms to conduct and coordinate operations will improve with the introduction of new onboard and offboard weapon, communication, and sensor systems. For example, the Navy's compact very lightweight torpedo (CVLWT) is a short-range weapon less than a third the size of the Mk-48 heavyweight torpedo; it could be used as a self-defense weapon on submarines or employed by large UUVs quiet enough to carry them close to targets. Similarly, small UAVs such as the Experimental Fuel Cell (XFC) UAV have relatively short endurance but can be launched by submarines or UUVs close to adversary coasts. They can take advantage of continued miniaturization in electro-optical, infrared, and radar sensors to conduct surveillance or electronic warfare missions.

Communications are a longstanding vulnerability of undersea platforms. New or improved undersea communication methods will likely enable undersea platforms to communicate with each other, systems on the ocean floor, and the larger joint force without having to expose a mast. Acoustic communications are increasingly able to operate over operationally relevant distances with low bandwidth, while at shorter ranges LEDs and lasers can achieve nearly the same data rates as wired systems. And new floating or towed radio transceivers enable submerged platforms to communicate with forces above the surface without risking detection.

The same power, communication, and processing advancements that are benefitting ASW capabilities and UUVs are making possible a growing variety of deployable payloads that sit on the sea-bed or float in the water column. For example, payloads like the Forward Deployed Energy and Communication Outpost (FDECO) can act as a rest stop for UUVs where they can download data and upload orders while recharging their batteries. The DARPA Upward Falling Payload (UFP) program is building a module that holds missiles or UAVs. And portable sensors such as the Shallow Water Surveillance System (SWSS) and Persistent Littoral Surveillance (PLUS) system can be placed in areas such as chokepoints where adversary submarines or UUVs are likely to travel.

The Next Chapter in Undersea Competition

While undersea research and development has been a distinct U.S. military advantage since the end of WWII, the wide availability of new processing and sensor technology and the increased exploitation of ocean resources are making undersea expertise more broadly available. This will result in increased undersea competition, even as U.S. forces are likely to retain a significant advantage for the next one to two decades. Some operational features of this competition are:

- A new predominant sensing technology. The effectiveness of traditional passive sonar will decline as submarines become quieter, their stealth is enhanced with countermeasures, and rivals deploy more unmanned systems that radiate little noise. While ASW relied primarily on passive sonar for the last 50 years, the dominant detection method by the 2020s may be low-frequency active sonar, non-acoustic detection, or some other previously unexploited technique made possible by ongoing technological advances.

- Undersea families of systems. Submarines will increasingly need to shift from being front-line tactical platforms like aircraft to being host and coordination platforms like aircraft carriers. Large UUVs and other deployed systems that are smaller and less detectable could increasingly be used instead of manned submarines for tactical missions close to enemy shores including coastal intelligence gathering, surveillance, mining, or electronic warfare.

- Undersea "battle networks." New longer-range sensors and emerging undersea communication capabilities will enable undersea fire control network operations analogous to those that use radio signals above the surface of the water. Undersea networks could also enable coordinated surveillance or attack operations by swarms of UUVs operating autonomously or controlled from a manned submarine or other platform.

- Seabed warfare: U.S. forces will need more immediately available undersea capacity inside areas contested by adversary surface and air A2/AD networks.

Deployed and fixed sensors, payload modules, and UUVs supported by systems like FDECO could augment U.S. submarine capacity and be managed by them during a conflict. Increased reliance on these capabilities will create a competition in the ability to place or eliminate systems on the coastal seabed, including capabilities for rapidly surveying and assessing the sea floor.

How the U.S. Navy should respond

The U.S. Navy is already developing new technologies and operational concepts to prepare for the emerging era in undersea warfare. These efforts will need to transition into acquisition programs and fielded capabilities, however, to sustain America's undersea advantage. The Navy should consider the following actions:

- Achieve organizational alignment: Submarines, UUVs, and fixed and deployable sonars are funded and managed by different headquarters, divisions, and separate acquisition organizations within the Navy. To ensure the performance characteristics, networking requirements, and development schedules of these programs are aligned, the Navy should make its undersea warfare resource sponsor and acquisition organizations responsible for all undersea vehicles and systems once they transition out of research and development.

- Ensure ballistic missile submarine (SSBN) survivability: Sound silencing will likely decrease in importance as U.S. noise reduction efforts reach an affordable limit and new ASW detection techniques, such as low-frequency active sonar, become more common. While becoming noisier is not an option, since passive sonar will still exist, the design for the next SSBN should address other ASW capabilities through the use of onboard and offboard systems and tactics.

- Establish UUV design priorities: The Department of Defense (DoD) has pursued a large variety of UUVs during the past decade, mostly for mine clearing and ocean surveillance, launched from surface ships or shore. These applications did not require particular sizes of UUVs. As UUVs become more integrated with submarines as part of a family of systems, the Navy should focus on UUVs that can use the submarine's ocean interfaces and conduct the most likely UUV missions. Specifically, the Navy should pursue the following UUV types as part of its undersea family of systems:

  o *Micro UUVs* (about 6" or less in diameter) are inexpensive and improving in their endurance and on-board power. They could be procured and deployed in large numbers or swarms as weapons, to survey the ocean floor, or to interfere with enemy ASW operations.

  o *Small UUVs* (about 12" in diameter) are commonly used today for surveys and minehunting, such as the Navy's Mk-18 UUV. They will be able to take on other surveillance or attack missions as part of the Fleet Modular Autonomous Undersea Vehicle (FMAUV) program and operate from submarines as well as surface ships and aircraft.

- *Medium UUVs* (about 21" in diameter) are the size of the Navy's Mk-48 submarine-launched torpedo. And while the Navy is not operating UUVs of this size today, the Modular Heavyweight Undersea Vehicle (MHUV) program plans to make the torpedo of the future able to be configured to conduct a range of missions, from mining and long-range attack to electronic warfare.

  - *Large UUVs* (about 80" in diameter) such as the Navy's Large Displacement UUV (LDUUV) are designed to use the planned Virginia Payload Module (VPM) tubes in Block V *Virginia*-class submarines. The LDUUV will provide a way for submarines to increase their sensor reach, expand their payload capacity, or deliver payloads into areas that are too risky or constrained for the submarine to reach.

  - *Extra-Large UUVs* (More than 80" in diameter) in development would be designed to launch from shore or very large ships with well decks or "moon pools." They could be used for long-endurance surveillance missions or primarily as "trucks" to deliver other payloads and UUVs. Experience with LDUUV will help inform concepts for using XLUUV.

- Evolve attack submarines (SSN) for their new roles: Submarines will be central to the future family of undersea systems and their design should reflect submarines' growing use as host and command and control platforms. The Navy should have a plan for evolving the existing *Los Angeles, Seawolf,* and *Virginia*-class submarines to incorporate features that expand their payload capacity and ability to interface with unmanned systems. This plan should also ensure the Block V *Virginia* submarines are able to host a wide range of payloads in addition to strike missiles.

- Move from research to acquisition: As described above, the Navy is very actively pursuing new undersea capabilities and demonstrating them at sea. But these new systems and concepts are slow to make it into acquisition. Several projects over the last decade including the Mission Reconfigurable UUV, Advanced Deployable System, and Deep Water Active Deployable System were prototyped but never fielded. The Navy cannot continue to delay the transition of new undersea systems into wider operational use.

The coming era in undersea competition will require a reconsideration of how military forces conduct undersea warfare. In particular, a new family of undersea vehicles and systems will be essential to exploit the undersea environment. If the United States does not begin fielding this new family soon, it could fall behind rivals who will field their own new technologies and operational concepts to threaten America's use of the undersea.

Mr. Bryan Clark

Prior to joining CSBA in 2013, Bryan Clark was Special Assistant to the Chief of Naval Operations and Director of his Commander's Action Group, where he led development of Navy strategy and implemented new initiatives in electromagnetic spectrum operations, undersea warfare, expeditionary operations and personnel and readiness management.

Mr. Clark served in the Navy headquarters staff from 2004 to 2011, leading studies in the Assessment Division and participating in the 2006 and 2010 Quadrennial Defense Reviews. His areas of emphasis were modeling and simulation, strategic planning and institutional reform and governance. Prior to retiring from the Navy in 2007, Mr. Clark was an enlisted and officer submariner, serving in afloat and ashore submarine operational and training assignments including tours as Chief Engineer and Operations Officer at the Navy's nuclear power training unit. Mr. Clark holds a Master of Science in National Security Studies from the National War College and a Bachelor of Science in Chemistry and Philosophy from the University of Idaho. He is the recipient of the Department of the Navy Superior Service Medal and the Legion of Merit.

DISCLOSURE FORM FOR WITNESSES
COMMITTEE ON ARMED SERVICES
U.S. HOUSE OF REPRESENTATIVES

INSTRUCTION TO WITNESSES: Rule 11, clause 2(g)(5), of the Rules of the U.S. House of Representatives for the 114th Congress requires nongovernmental witnesses appearing before House committees to include in their written statements a curriculum vitae and a disclosure of the amount and source of any federal contracts or grants (including subcontracts and subgrants), or contracts or payments originating with a foreign government, received during the current and two previous calendar years either by the witness or by an entity represented by the witness and related to the subject matter of the hearing. This form is intended to assist witnesses appearing before the House Committee on Armed Services in complying with the House rule. Please note that a copy of these statements, with appropriate redactions to protect the witness's personal privacy (including home address and phone number) will be made publicly available in electronic form not later than one day after the witness's appearance before the committee. Witnesses may list additional grants, contracts, or payments on additional sheets, if necessary.

Witness name: Bryan Clark

Capacity in which appearing: (check one)

◯ Individual

◉ Representative

If appearing in a representative capacity, name of the company, association or other entity being represented: Center for Strategic and Budgetary Assessments

Federal Contract or Grant Information: If you or the entity you represent before the Committee on Armed Services has contracts (including subcontracts) or grants (including subgrants) with the federal government, please provide the following information:

2015

Federal grant/ contract	Federal agency	Dollar value	Subject of contract or grant
W91QF0-15-P-0010	Army War College	$55,000	Strategic Choices exercise
HQ0034-14-D-0017	OSD/ONA	$1,700,000	Multiple delivery orders
HQ0034-15-P-0136	WHA-Acquisition Directorate	$72,475	Secretary of Defense Corporate Fellows Program
FA8650-15-C-7570	DARPA	$714,912	Developing & Improving Transition of System of System Technology

2014

Federal grant/ contract	Federal agency	Dollar value	Subject of contract or grant
SP4705-10-C-0019	National Defense University	$86,000	Secretary of Defense Corporate Fellows program
N00189-13-F-Z085	Department of the Navy	$120,987	Portfolio Rebalancing Exercise
HR0011-14-C-0112	DARPA	$252,778	System of Systems Transition study
HQ0034-09-D-3007	OSD/ONA	2,136,487	Multiple delivery orders

2013

Federal grant/ contract	Federal agency	Dollar value	Subject of contract or grant
HR0011-13-C-0028	DARPA	$174,939	Battle Network Competitions study
SP4705-10-C-0019	National Defense University	$84,000	Secretary of Defense Corporate Fellows program
HQ0034-09-D-3007	OSD/ONA	$1,200,000	Multiple delivery orders
W91QF0-13-P-0029	Army War College	$62,890	Portfolio Rebalancing Exercise
W91QF0-14-P-0013	Army War College	$57,915	Portfolio Rebalancing Exercise
GS-10F-022AA	National Commission on the Structure of the Air Force	$74,728	Portfolio Rebalancing and Strategic Analysis

<u>Foreign Government Contract or Payment Information</u>: If you or the entity you represent before the Committee on Armed Services has contracts or payments originating from a foreign government, please provide the following information:

2015

Foreign contract/ payment	Foreign government	Dollar value	Subject of contract or payment
Embassy of Japan	Japan	$110,000	Defense Planning Seminar

2014

Foreign contract/ payment	Foreign government	Dollar value	Subject of contract or payment
Embassy of Japan	Japan	$100,000	Defense Planning Seminar
UAE	UAE	$125,000	Regional Security workshops
Embassy of Japan	Japan	$30,000	Meetings and briefings

2013

Foreign contract/ payment	Foreign government	Dollar value	Subject of contract or payment
Embassy of Japan	Japan	$100,000	Defense Planning Seminar
Embassy of Japan	Japan	$30,000	Meetings and briefings

QUESTIONS SUBMITTED BY MEMBERS POST HEARING

OCTOBER 27, 2015

Mr. LANGEVIN. I noted with interest the testimony regarding the need to develop a common battlespace picture of the undersea, regardless of the platforms and individual sensor inputs. What would this look like in your mind, what are the linchpin technologies and concepts that would need to be developed in order to enable this system of systems, and are we currently designing sensors and systems with the ability to communicate in such a way?

Admiral CONNOR. In my mind, the solution would have a background that looked like "Google Earth" and then have multiple layers of data that could be layered on top of that background. Each layer would represent a different source of data and each layer could be at a different classification level, with the classification varying as a function of the sensitivity of the data source. Users would be authorized to see all of the data that they are cleared for, subject also to the classification level of the room in which is was displayed.

The technologies exist today and consist of tagging information from various sources with a geographic position, a time stamp, a source identifier, and other metadata as needed. There is no particular sensor technology required here. A good battle space picture will be able to accept data from a variety of sources.

It should be noted that systems with the proper characteristics are being introduced at some of the intelligence agencies. My point for DOD is that these technologies need to be standardized across the Department of Defense and used in the operations centers where tactical and operational level decisions are made. Unfortunately, the command centers on our ships and in our fleet headquarters do not effectively leverage this technology today. As a result, the speed and quality of operational decisions will continue to suffer until this is overcome.

To get a sense of how the technology exists in the private sector today, just look at a Google map and select the layers of information that you wish to display such as weather, traffic, restaurant locations etc. We should have the ability to do something like this with a chart of the ocean, then layer AIS traffic, weather, satellite derived intelligence, reports from our ships, reports from fixed sensors, and so forth. That does not exist today in a simple, standard format that could be shared across the Joint Force.

Mr. LANGEVIN. I appreciated your testimony about the need for nonspecific innovation funding and broadly defined programs. While I agree about the need for increased agility and freedom to fail on innovative ideas, this concept always comes into significant tension with the need for Congressional oversight and accountability. Can you provide examples of programs besides APB/TI that have been defined properly, in your view, and ones that have not? Are there innovation funds elsewhere in the budget that you would use as a model?

Admiral CONNOR. There are specific innovation funds that are controlled by the Department of Defense Strategic Capabilities Office. This represents a good start. As we also discussed in testimony, there are Speed to Fleet funds controlled by the Office of Naval Research. However, as I noted in testimony, the time frame for deciding how to allocate Speed to Fleet funds takes about a year, defeating the intent of the program.

In addition to the APB/TI process used in the submarine combat system, there is more a more recent program in the Aegis combat system called the Advanced Capabilities Build (ACB) program that has migrated that system much closer to an easy to modernize, Commercial Off the Shelf (COTS) strategy that should be able to handle change more easily in the future than in the past.

An example of a program that has struggled to incorporate technology is the LCS mine countermeasures mission package. This package is derived from a program that was originally conceived to deploy from an aircraft carrier. Is is based on a diesel powered Remote Minehunting System (RMS) that tows an acoustic sensor (AQS–20) I don't have access to the entire history of the program, but believe it to be about of 20 years old. It has yet to deliver a meaningful capability. In the interim, the field of autonomous undersea vehicles (AUV) has emerged and offered solutions that have been deployed as prototypes in the Arabian Gulf. The AUV-based programs will likely overtake the LCS mine countermeasures program of record. The

Navy struggles as an institution to make a decision such as abandoning a non-performing program with significant sunk costs in favor of a more elegant solution that uses more modern technology. Part of that difficulty involves the need to go to Congress and report "failure." My point here is that recognizing that a solution is obsolete and cutting (or restructuring) the underlying program in favor of better technology should not be considered failure. It should be considered an appropriate business decision.

I would like address your accountability concerns. I agree that there is a tension between freedom to innovate and proper stewardship of taxpayer dollars. However, our current system focuses the accountability at the level of the program manager and below. Program managers are incentivized by initiatives such as Nunn-McCurdy to set modest goals and then meet those goals as inexpensively as possible. As a result, a program with a long lead time will often reject technology that becomes available after those goals were set due to either the administrative obstacles or financial hurdles, even if that technology could make that system much more effective. This can result in programs that meet program goals, but do not deliver capability that is still relevant at the time of delivery.

While program managers are accountable to meet the goals of their program, there is no senior officer or senior civilian accountability for ensuring that the program goals actually provide the capabilities we will need to prevail in time of war. For example, there is no bureaucratic tension or accountability over the fact that potential adversaries have as anti-ship missiles with engagement ranges greater than our own. This is a significant problem that will limit the manner in which we will be able to deploy our surface ships in time of war.

Congressional oversight and accountability of senior leaders to ensure that they have a viable overall strategy and an agile means of delivering the capabilities that enable strategy is an important counterweight to oversight at the program level.

Mr. LANGEVIN. In your opinion, are we investing enough in the enabling technologies for next-generations sensors—communications, advanced processing, and other sensor-independent areas—as well as the potential sensors themselves to position ourselves well on the sensing and communications side for the battle network competitions of the future? What would your "next dollar" go to? And are there investments that we are making now that risk being stranded?

Admiral CONNOR. In the area of enabling technologies, I think there are opportunities to do better. In the near term, I would focus on the underlying technologies that would help us get more out of the sensors that we have.

I would focus first on machine learning. We need this technology to do more acoustic analysis onboard unmanned systems and even in the headquarters where a large number of systems will feed the overall picture. Historically, each acoustic sensor system required a person to review the live information stream produced by that sensor and make an assessment regarding the information presented. This method of analysis will not be tenable if we succeed in placing larger numbers of inexpensive sensors in the field. There have been previous attempts at "automatic target classification" that have failed in the past. However, we now have more elegant methods available in which the machine actually learns its environment and recognizes changes with little human interaction. Success in this area will make us more effective and much more efficient.

Other focus areas that would help us move forward more effectively include covert communications, undersea fiber optic networks, and charging stations for unmanned vehicles. These technologies will help us share the information that we gather more effectively and keep our autonomous sensors on the front line longer.

Mr. LANGEVIN. Mr. Clark testified to the need to organizationally realign the Navy to bring the undersea under a single roof. Do you agree with his suggestion? What in your view would be the optimal organizational structure for the undersea?

Admiral CONNOR. I do not agree with his suggestion. The current system in which the service is organized around the major warfare communities serves a good purpose. It allows the community leaders to focus with an expert staff on acquisition issues, community management, and educational issues necessary to the healthy functioning of those communities. Also, each warfare community fights as part of a Joint Team in strike warfare, surface warfare, undersea warfare and special operations. Warriors from each community need to be broad enough to work across undersea/surface/strike warfare because all of the warfare communities support all of these missions in war time.

To the extent that some organizational change may be necessary to adapt to future security requirements, the recent establishment of N99, an OPNAV division to support unmanned systems, is a good step. It recognizes that there is a growing unmanned element to each major warfare area.

The Navy needs a mind-set change more than it needs an organizational change. The change involves recognition that we are already in a world in which military superiority will be determined by the speed of innovation. Our military peer competitors are innovating at a faster pace than us. We struggle to move forward technologically because our budget cycle and acquisition cycles are longer than those of our rivals and are a root cause of the declining margin in our superiority—including undersea superiority. The navy (and the other services) are not pushing hard enough to create an environment in which pace of innovation is recognized as a strategic asset.

Mr. LANGEVIN. I noted with interest the testimony regarding the need to develop a common battlespace picture of the undersea, regardless of the platforms and individual sensor inputs. What would this look like in your mind, what are the linchpin technologies and concepts that would need to be developed in order to enable this system of systems, and are we currently designing sensors and systems with the ability to communicate in such a way?

Mr. CLARK. The undersea common operational picture (COP) will be different than the COP that can be created using sensors and networks above the water. Sonar and non-acoustic undersea sensors are less precise and accurate than radar or electro-optical systems. As a result, the undersea COP will often consist of approximate target positions and classifications along with an estimate of their accuracy, or an "area of uncertainty." And because undersea communications have much lower bandwidth than radiofrequency (RF) systems above the water, the undersea COP will take longer to develop and update.

The limitations inherent in establishing an undersea COP, however, may not significantly hinder undersea operations. Unmanned undersea vehicles (UUV) and submarines travel slower than about 35 knots in all conditions, and less than about 15 knots to maintain their acoustic stealth. Their positions will not change quickly, and they are unlikely to inadvertently move into a higher threat area or risk a collision with another vehicle due to an imprecise operational picture.

The key role of undersea networks

The networks that create an undersea operational picture will be different than those above water and are largely limited by physics rather than technology. Because RF signals in the frequencies U.S. forces most often used for communication travel only a few feet in water, undersea communication networks will rely on a combination of acoustic, fiber optic, RF, and laser or LED-based communication systems to connect commanders ashore with undersea forces inside contested or denied areas.

Fiber optic and RF communication systems will form the "long-haul" portion of the network between main operating bases in the United States or overseas and the edge of friendly waters. These systems will terminate at gateway buoys or underwater nodes that translate RF or fiber optic communications into acoustic or laser/LED signals. Fiber optic cable networks on the ocean floor could be combined with undersea sonar arrays to enable a single system to act both as part of the sensor network and as the communication backbone.

Physics and the operating environment will dictate whether acoustic or laser/LED communications are best used to connect operating undersea forces with fiber optic or RF networks that can only reach the edge of denied areas. Laser/LED or medium frequency (1,000–10,000 hertz) acoustic transmitters can communicate over a distance of a few hundred yards with the speed of a slow internet connection. Acoustic transducers at low frequencies (less than 1,000 hertz) can reach up to about 100 miles away, but with transmission rates of less than 1000 bits per second, it will take minutes to send each message. As with RF communications, the bandwidth of acoustic and light-based undersea communications changes with their frequency, whereas the range of acoustic communications is changes inversely with their frequency. The farther communications need to go, the less data can be sent and a message will take longer to send. Long-range communications will be relatively slow, and short-range ones will be faster.

Submarines and unmanned systems operating relatively close to RF or fiber gateways can use acoustic and laser/LED communications to connect to the network. For undersea forces that are far from fiber optic cables and unable to expose themselves to use RF communications, the bandwidth and range limitations associated with acoustic and laser/LED communications may make relays the most efficient way to connect with commanders and support organizations ashore. These relays, such as the Navy's Forward Deployed Energy and Communication Outpost (FDECO) program, can be deployed on the sea floor, act as energy and communication stations that collect messages going to and from UUVs or submarines, and communicate with undersea gateways in friendly waters using long-range acoustic communications or UUV "data mules" that physically carry information in onboard computer memory. These stations can also recharge UUVs and themselves be recharged by the data mules.

The key technologies needed to put these undersea networks in place are long-range acoustic and short-range laser/LED communication systems, deployable and fixed fiber optic cable communication networks, processing capabilities, and deployable communication and energy station. The Navy is developing these technologies through numerous basic science and applied research programs, and most are mature. The most significant gap is in communication processing technology; undersea communications will operate at widely varying levels of bandwidth and latency, and synchronizing inputs and outputs will require new signal processing software and hardware.

Despite its work in technology, the Navy is not aggressively pursuing programs that will demonstrate these technologies in operationally relevant situations such as the Undersea Constellation and FDECO. The Navy should put together a plan for the development of its future undersea battle networks and demonstration of these capabilities at sea through programs that can be transitioned into the DOD acquisition system.

Importance of sensor technology

Because of the bandwidth and range limitations associated with undersea communications, UUVs and unmanned systems will not be remotely operated like unmanned air vehicles such as the MQ–1 Predator and MQ–9 Reaper. They will need to be largely autonomous. Autonomy technology is improving quickly, and many new UUVs and other unmanned undersea systems are able to select missions from a prioritized list of tasks and re-task themselves in response to new information.

The quality of sensor information and analysis, however, will be the most significant constraint on autonomy. The emerging generation of UUVs are able to travel safely to a prescribed location, avoid hazards such as ships and debris, follow applicable navigation rules and regulations, and execute simple tasks such as survey the bottom or deploy mines. For these operations UUVs and unmanned systems do not need a high level of certainty regarding the position of the UUV or system, as well as the location and classification of contacts around it.

Unmanned undersea systems could also be used for responsive operations such as attacking enemy ships or submarines. These operations will require a high level of certainty regarding the position and classification of a contact the unmanned system will attack, because it will not be controlled by a human operator who can be accountable for taking the risk of attacking a contact based on uncertain sensor information. As a result, the unmanned system will often not engage, missing opportunities to achieve the undersea force's military objectives. Without better sensors and target recognition capabilities, UUVs will remain constrained to missions where the target or location can be very precisely and accurately determined.

The Navy is developing new undersea sensor technologies that will enable U.S. forces to detect enemy submarines at longer ranges and classify them more accurately. This work should continue and emphasize the ability of unmanned systems, including UUVs, to characterize the threat environment and act autonomously in response. Some programs, such as the Persistent Littoral Undersea Surveillance (PLUS) system, have been effective at enabling an unmanned system to detect and roughly classify undersea contacts. More demonstrations of this type should be conducted to refine this technology so future unmanned systems will be able to fully exploit ongoing advances in autonomy.

Mr. LANGEVIN. In your opinion, are we investing enough in the enabling technologies for next-generations sensors—communications, advanced processing, and other sensor-independent areas—as well as the potential sensors themselves to position ourselves well on the sensing and communications side for the battle network competitions of the future? What would your "next dollar" go to? And are there investments that we are making now that risk being stranded?

Mr. CLARK. The Navy is making appropriate investments in new sensor, communication, networking, and data processing technologies. They are not, however, devoting enough money or effort toward transitioning the most useful of these technologies into operationally useful systems by incorporating them into acquisition programs or demonstrating them with prototype projects in the fleet. The lack of priority and selectivity in undersea system development is largely due to the lack of operational concepts describing how the Navy will conduct future undersea operations. New or modified requirements are based on new operational concepts and, in turn, drive the development of new acquisition programs.

There are several key new operational concepts the Navy should analyze to determine if they should drive new systems and systems of systems, such as:

- Low Frequency Active (LFA) Sonar Anti-Submarine Warfare (ASW): The Navy's current ASW concepts center on the use of passive sonar to detect and track the noise emanating from an enemy submarine. This technique depends on the adversary making noise, which became increasing difficult in the late Cold War as the Soviets incorporated sound-silencing technology into their submarines. This challenge will eventually return as Chinese, Russian, and other nation's submarines improve. Further, passive sonar cannot generally detect enemy submarines outside the range of submarine-launched anti-ship missiles, leaving U.S. surface ships vulnerable to an unwarned attack.

  The Navy needs to consider approaches for surface and air ASW that use LFA sonar, such as in the Littoral Combat Ship (LCS) Variable Depth Sonar (VDS) and the Compact LFA array onboard the Navy's civilian-crewed ocean surveillance (T-AGOS) ship. LFA sonar offers longer detection ranges than passive sonar that can exceed the range of submarine-launched missiles and can translate into greater search areas and faster searches. New concepts could also include the use of LFA sonars on unmanned systems or UUVs that detect submarines and communicate their location to other platforms, or simply drive them away from certain areas. Submarines detected with LFA sonar would then be prosecuted with more accurate passive sensors, or engaged with standoff weapons such as missiles equipped with small torpedoes or depth bombs. While the Navy has some of the technologies needed for these concepts in the fleet or in development, it lacks some pieces of the LFA ASW "kill chain," specifically long-range standoff ASW weapons, unmanned LFA systems, and LFA sensors for combatant ships other than LCS.

- Passive ASW by unmanned systems: Passive sonar detection ranges are less than those of submarine-launched weapons, and this situation will get worse as adversaries become quieter. Passive sonar should therefore move increasingly onto unmanned systems which are not as vulnerable to counterattack and which can use emerging undersea battle networks to pass contact information to manned or unmanned forces that can prosecute submarine contacts. Further, the capability of a passive sonar array varies with the size of the sonar array, with larger arrays providing greater range and sensitivity. Large arrays are difficult to place on a manned or unmanned platform, but could be incorporated into a deployable or fixed stationary unmanned sensor system such as the Navy's Sound Surveillance System (SOSUS) arrays positioned at key chokepoints overseas and around the U.S. coast.

  The Navy needs to expand on SOSUS and similar fixed systems by developing more deployable passive arrays that can be placed at chokepoints, around enemy ports, and adjacent to friendly bases. These systems, depending on their design, can also provide the fiber optic power and communication backbone to connect undersea forces with commanders and support organizations ashore using laser, LED, or acoustic communication gateways. Examples of these arrays include PLUS, the Reliable Acoustic Path (RAP) Vertical Line Array (VLA), and the Shallow Water Surveillance System (SWSS), all of which have been challenged with uncertain funding and support over the last decade. But, as with LFA sonar ASW techniques, the enabling technologies for these approaches are mature; they just have to make it across the technology "valley of death" into acquisition programs.

- Counter-UUV technologies: Not much work has been done on how to prevent enemy UUVs from attacking U.S. infrastructure or ships. As UUV and undersea battle network technologies improve and become more widely available, the Navy will need to be able to protect high-value targets in the homeland and abroad. Traditional ASW approaches will likely not work well against militarized UUVs due to their small size and ability to have low radiated noise. New sensor technologies, such as high frequency sonar, and passive and active defensive systems will be needed to defeat them.

- Power projection from undersea unmanned systems: The anti-access capabilities proliferating today above the surface will soon expand to include undersea surveillance and attack systems in areas adjacent to enemy coasts. The Navy will need to develop concepts for conducting surveillance, strike, anti-ship, or cyber/ electronic warfare operations from unmanned systems to avoid placing manned submarines in high-risk areas.

  The key enabling technologies for these concepts include undersea battle networks to support communications between manned submarines and unmanned systems, as well as between submarines and commanders or support organizations ashore (as described in Question 5 above); sensor and contact recognition technologies for unmanned systems; a family of UUVs for various roles; weapons and other payloads that can be deployed by unmanned systems; and power technologies to enable extended unmanned system operations. There are improvements the Navy could make in each of these areas. The need for placing emphasis on battle network signal processing, demonstrations of signal processing technology, and better contact recognition for unmanned systems are described above.

Regarding UUVs, the Navy as been favoring small ones, such as the approximately 12-inch diameter Mk-18 UUV that ordnance disposal and oceanographic researchers use, and the new Large Displacement UUV (LDUUV) that could be launched from the Virginia Payload Module (VPM) tube. The Navy needs to accelerate its efforts to deploy the 21-inch diameter Modular Heavyweight Underwater Vehicle (MHUV) that will be the size of its current Mk-48 torpedo and use many parts of that weapon. The MHUV will enable a variety of long-range surveillance, strike, and anti-ship operations from submarines that will give them greater standoff capability from threat areas and leverage existing systems and technology. The Navy also needs to increase its research into applications for micro UUVs that are less than six inches in diameter and three to four feet long. New power technologies are enabling these UUVs to achieve ranges and endurance that would make "swarm" operations possible in which large numbers of expendable and inexpensive micro UUVs conduct surveillance or attack missions that would otherwise require a much larger reusable vehicle or a submarine.

Future power projection operations undersea will establish a need for undersea lift, similar to the lift used for amphibious forces above the surface. Payloads such as energy and communication relays, mines, sensor arrays, and other stationary unmanned systems will need to be placed in proximity to enemy coasts or at key chokepoints. For example, DARPA is developing the Upward Falling Payload and HYDRA programs, both of which provide ways of placing payloads on the sea floor. The Navy, however, may not have enough submarines to support future undersea lift operations, or they may not want to place manned submarines at risk to conduct them. The Navy should therefore explore the use of extra-large UUVs (XLUUV) for deploying larger|payloads. These UUVs would be launched from shore or large vessels, such as amphibious ships, and have ranges of more than 1000 miles and endurance of six months or more. In addition to lift operations, XLUUVs could also conduct long-term surveillance missions that would otherwise require a submarine to be on station for months at a time.

Conducting undersea lift operations will require that submarines and larger UUVs have systems such as the Universal Launch and Recovery Module (ULRM) that enable deployment and recovery (when needed) of payloads. This system is being developed today for the VPM tube, but variants of it could be used in the future on larger UUVs and by undersea payload modules that deploy smaller UUVs.

The Navy is developing several weapons, unmanned aerial vehicles (UAVs), and other payloads that could be deployed by unmanned systems. This effort needs to be more organized and guided by new operational concepts that describe how unmanned systems will contribute to undersea power projection operations and take advantage of new technologies for miniaturization of weapon guidance systems and warheads. For example, UUVs can themselves be mines or carry mines to a deployment area with today's level of sensor capability and autonomy. The Navy, however, is not aggressively developing mine payloads for UUVs and is slowly advancing the MHUV (which could likewise be a mine or carry small mines). Similarly, the Navy has experimented with small UAVs being deployed from submarines, but has not yet devised a concept for deploying them from UUVs or for using undersea-launched UAVs in power projection or surveillance operations.

These are the most significant operational concepts the Navy should be developing and analyzing as the basis behind new requirements for undersea systems. Operational concepts are essential for identifying the most important new technologies and systems to pursue, and to establish requirements for future acquisition programs.

I would recommend the next dollar in undersea system development funding go to completing and demonstrating the undersea battle network. It is the fundamental capability that will enable UUVs, unmanned systems, and submarines to work together to sustain the ability of the Navy to project power from the undersea and deny enemies from doing the same. After that, funding is needed most urgently for counter-UUV technologies, XL and micro UUVs, the ULRM, and small UUV-launched payloads.

Mr. LANGEVIN. In your testimony, you mention the concept that manned submarines could become conceptually closer to aircraft carriers through the employment of UUVs and coordination of families of systems. What, in your view, is holding us back from realizing this vision? Is it payload space, autonomy programming, policy limitations, communications, technology maturity, or something else?

Mr. CLARK. There are four elements which need to be addressed in order for the Navy to shift manned submarines from being only front-line tactical platforms to being operational level platforms controlling a wider undersea force:

- Payload volume: Submarines will be, for the foreseeable future, the most secure and accurate means of delivering unmanned systems and UUVs to their deployment areas. Although XLUUVs and LDUUVs will be able to take on some of this lift mission, they will not provide the level of adaptability to changing circumstances, certainty of deployment, and security against counter-detection as a submarine. This makes VPM tubes or something like them critical in future submarines.
- Communication and command and control capabilities: As described in Questions 5 and 6, undersea battle networks using laser/LED and acoustic communications are essential to connect shore bases, submarines, and unmanned systems. Submarines, for their part, will need a greater number and variety of communication systems to interface with this network. In many situations, real-time communications with commanders ashore will not be possible due to the low bandwidth of long-range acoustic communications. Therefore, submarine commanders will be in charge of their local manned and unmanned undersea systems. This will require communication and planning capabilities similar to a large combatant such as an aircraft carrier or cruiser.
- Submarine-compatible UUVs and UAVs: The Navy is developing the LDUUV, MHUV, and interfaces for the Mk-18 UUV to be launched from a submarine torpedo tube. The Navy should also be developing micro UUVs and interfaces so they can be deployed from the submarine three-inch launcher or in larger numbers from torpedo tubes, VPM tubes, or by MHUVs. To exploit the potential in small UAVs, the Navy should also develop small UAVs that can be carried and launched in large numbers from submarines or larger UUVs.
- Launch and recovery systems: Submarines will need mechanisms such as the ULRM to deploy and recover unmanned systems and UUVs as well as the means to deploy UAVs.

QUESTIONS SUBMITTED BY MR. COOK

Mr. COOK. Is U.S. industry ready to deliver the systems and components needed in a competitive and robust way? Has the Navy insured that the industrial base, the talent pool, the pipeline of industry investment is in the condition needed to deliver? What can Congress do to ensure these components are in place?

Admiral CONNOR. The Navy has done well to sustain the legacy industrial base in areas such as ship building and aircraft production. Although it is very expensive to so, it is necessary because the country has no viable large commercial ship building companies and only one viable large scale commercial aircraft manufacturer. The shipbuilding industry in particular is undergoing tremendous work force change as older employees approach retirement age. The Navy has supported efforts to train the next generation of workers in both public and private shipyards.

Congress can help by supporting a steady production rate with long term contracts. These contracts allow prime contractors, subcontractors and suppliers to make long term decisions to build and retain a sustainable work force.

The Navy and the DOD have not done very well in leveraging the talent that resides in the more dynamic areas of our economy. Most of the innovation that takes place in the United States is accomplished by small companies using private funds. These companies often avoid building products and services for purely governmental functions because they perceive that it is too hard to work with government as a customer. Therefore, we tend to give most of our business to a declining number of companies that know us well and with which we have a long history. That could be a handicap, however, when it comes to sustaining the ability to repeatedly generate game changing innovations.

To leverage the most dynamic and innovative portion of our economy, the Department of Defense should move away from obtuse requirements of the Federal Acquisition Regulations and create a face for industry that looks and feels like any other commercial entity.

Mr. COOK. Is the Navy ready to employ these new technologies when they are delivered? Have the warfighters developed the Command and Control processes and procedures, the rules of use, the common operating pictures and methods needed to employ program of record delivered systems on the day they are delivered?

Admiral CONNOR. Our sailors are very adaptable and will not be the limiting factor in how quickly we leverage unmanned systems and exploit a better common operating picture. The Maritime Operations Centers established nearly navy-wide over the last 5 years or so have significantly increased Navy command and control capacity. Providing a better common operating picture and delivering more information from remote systems will leverage those improvements.

The Navy has processes such as table top exercises, fleet battle experiments, and large scale fleet exercises to gracefully integrate new capabilities as they become available.

Mr. COOK. Is U.S. industry ready to deliver the systems and components needed in a competitive and robust way? Has the Navy insured that the industrial base, the talent pool, the pipeline of industry investment is in the condition needed to deliver? What can Congress do to ensure these components are in place?

Mr. CLARK. The Navy has fostered a large and diverse base of small companies that develop unmanned systems, communication networks, and undersea payloads. These companies, however, will not be able to scale the production of these systems up to the level that will be needed to create future undersea battle networks and implement new concepts for ASW, surveillance, and power projection from undersea. For example, the Navy plans to restart the Mk-48 torpedo production line, which will likely be a key element in developing and producing the new MHUV UUV. The companies bidding on the torpedo restart, however, will likely be small companies that may not be able to support expanded production of Mk-48 components needed for the MHUV. Similarly, Navy's deployable sensor arrays, small UUVs, and UUV-deployable payloads are being developed and built at prototype scale by university laboratories and small firms that will not able to build these systems in large numbers.

Making large-scale production of new undersea systems feasible will require incentivizing larger industry partners to build them by establishing requirements and acquisition programs that focus investment on a smaller number of the most useful systems. The Navy is in a position to do this now, given its knowledge and experience with undersea systems and emerging operational concepts for future undersea operations. Congress can help by influencing the Navy to make these investment choices and by providing an opportunity to focus its investment by adjusting the proposed President's budget during the appropriations process. This normally happens a year after the budget was developed within the Navy, and Navy officials and analysts likely have new insights to better guide spending decisions.

A significant concern going forward is the nation's talent pool in engineering and physics, which form the bulk of technical expertise needed for development of undersea systems. Graduate students should be incentivized to go into physics and ocean, mechanical, and electrical engineering through funding of graduate education and opportunities to work in government research organizations.

Mr. COOK. Is the Navy ready to employ these new technologies when they are delivered? Have the warfighters developed the Command and Control processes and procedures, the rules of use, the common operating pictures and methods needed to employ program of record delivered systems on the day they are delivered?

Mr. CLARK. The Navy is making appropriate investments in new sensor, communication, networking, and data processing technologies. They are not, however, devoting enough money or effort toward transitioning the most useful of these technologies into operationally useful systems by incorporating them into acquisition programs or demonstrating them with prototype projects in the fleet. The lack of priority and selectivity in undersea system development is largely due to the lack of operational concepts describing how the Navy will conduct future undersea operations. New or modified requirements are based on new operational concepts and, in turn, drive the development of new acquisition programs.

There are several key new operational concepts the Navy should analyze to determine if they should drive new systems and systems of systems, such as:

• Low Frequency Active (LFA) Sonar Anti-Submarine Warfare (ASW): The Navy's current ASW concepts center on the use of passive sonar to detect and track the noise emanating from an enemy submarine. This technique depends on the adversary making noise, which became increasing difficult in the late Cold War as the Soviets incorporated sound-silencing technology into their submarines. This challenge will eventually return as Chinese, Russian, and other nation's submarines improve. Further, passive sonar cannot generally detect enemy submarines outside the range of submarine-launched anti-ship missiles, leaving U.S. surface ships vulnerable to an unwarned attack.

The Navy needs to consider approaches for surface and air ASW that use LFA sonar, such as in the Littoral Combat Ship (LCS) Variable Depth Sonar (VDS) and the Compact LFA array onboard the Navy's civilian-crewed ocean surveillance (T–AGOS) ship. LFA sonar offers longer detection ranges than passive sonar that can exceed the range of submarine-launched missiles and can translate into greater search areas and faster searches. New concepts could also include the use of LFA sonars on unmanned systems or UUVs that detect submarines and communicate their location to other platforms, or simply drive them away from certain areas. Submarines detected with LFA sonar would then be prosecuted with more accurate passive sensors, or engaged with standoff weapons such as missiles equipped with small torpedoes or depth bombs. While the Navy has some of the technologies needed for these concepts in the fleet or in development, it lacks some pieces of the LFA ASW "kill chain," specifically long-range standoff ASW weapons, unmanned LFA systems, and LFA sensors for combatant ships other than LCS.

- Passive ASW by unmanned systems: Passive sonar detection ranges are less than those of submarine-launched weapons, and this situation will get worse as adversaries become quieter. Passive sonar should therefore move increasingly onto unmanned systems which are not as vulnerable to counterattack and which can use emerging undersea battle networks to pass contact information to manned or unmanned forces that can prosecute submarine contacts. Further, the capability of a passive sonar array varies with the size of the sonar array, with larger arrays providing greater range and sensitivity. Large arrays are difficult to place on a manned or unmanned platform, but could be incorporated into a deployable or fixed stationary unmanned sensor system such as the Navy's Sound Surveillance System (SOSUS) arrays positioned at key chokepoints overseas and around the U.S. coast.

The Navy needs to expand on SOSUS and similar fixed systems by developing more deployable passive arrays that can be placed at chokepoints, around enemy ports, and adjacent to friendly bases. These systems, depending on their design, can also provide the fiber optic power and communication backbone to connect undersea forces with commanders and support organizations ashore using laser, LED, or acoustic communication gateways. Examples of these arrays include PLUS, the Reliable Acoustic Path (RAP) Vertical Line Array (VLA), and the Shallow Water Surveillance System (SWSS), all of which have been challenged with uncertain funding and support over the last decade. But, as with LFA sonar ASW techniques, the enabling technologies for these approaches are mature; they just have to make it across the technology "valley of death" into acquisition programs.

- Counter-UUV technologies: Not much work has been done on how to prevent enemy UUVs from attacking U.S. infrastructure or ships. As UUV and undersea battle network technologies improve and become more widely available, the Navy will need to be able to protect high-value targets in the homeland and abroad. Traditional ASW approaches will likely not work well against militarized UUVs due to their small size and ability to have low radiated noise. New sensor technologies, such as high frequency sonar, and passive and active defensive systems will be needed to defeat them.

- Power projection from undersea unmanned systems: The anti-access capabilities proliferating today above the surface will soon expand to include undersea surveillance and attack systems in areas adjacent to enemy coasts. The Navy will need to develop concepts for conducting surveillance, strike, anti-ship, or cyber/electronic warfare operations from unmanned systems to avoid placing manned submarines in high-risk areas.

The key enabling technologies for these concepts include undersea battle networks to support communications between manned submarines and unmanned systems, as well as between submarines and commanders or support organizations ashore (as described in Question 5 above); sensor and contact recognition technologies for unmanned systems; a family of UUVs for various roles; weapons and other payloads that can be deployed by unmanned systems; and power technologies to enable extended unmanned system operations. There are improvements the Navy could make in each of these areas. The need for placing emphasis on battle network signal processing, demonstrations of signal processing technology, and better contact recognition for unmanned systems are described above.

Regarding UUVs, the Navy as been favoring small ones, such as the approximately 12-inch diameter Mk-18 UUV that ordnance disposal and oceanographic researchers use, and the new Large Displacement UUV (LDUUV) that could be launched from the Virginia Payload Module (VPM) tube. The Navy needs to accelerate its efforts to deploy the 21-inch diameter Modular Heavyweight Underwater Vehicle (MHUV) that will be the size of its current Mk-48 torpedo and use many parts of that weapon. The MHUV will enable a variety of long-range surveillance, strike, and anti-ship operations from submarines that will give them greater standoff capability from threat areas and leverage existing systems and technology. The Navy also needs to increase its research into applications for micro UUVs that are less than six inches in diameter and three to four feet long. New power technologies are enabling these UUVs to achieve ranges and endurance that would make "swarm" operations possible in which large numbers of expendable and inexpensive micro UUVs conduct surveillance or attack missions that would otherwise require a much larger reusable vehicle or a submarine.

Future power projection operations undersea will establish a need for undersea lift, similar to the lift used for amphibious forces above the surface. Payloads such as energy and communication relays, mines, sensor arrays, and other stationary unmanned systems will need to be placed in proximity to enemy coasts or at key chokepoints. For example, DARPA is developing the Upward Falling Payload and HYDRA programs, both of which provide ways of placing payloads on the sea floor. The Navy, however, may not have enough submarines to support future undersea lift operations, or they may not want to place manned submarines at risk to conduct them. The Navy should therefore explore the use of extra-large UUVs (XLUUV) for deploying larger payloads. These UUVs would be launched from shore or large vessels, such as amphibious ships, and have ranges of more than 1000 miles and endurance of six months or more. In addition to lift operations, XLUUVs could also conduct long-term surveillance missions that would otherwise require a submarine to be on station for months at a time.

Conducting undersea lift operations will require that submarines and larger UUVs have systems such as the Universal Launch and Recovery Module (ULRM) that enable deployment and recovery (when needed) of payloads. This system is being developed today for the VPM tube, but variants of it could be used in the future on larger UUVs and by undersea payload modules that deploy smaller UUVs.

The Navy is developing several weapons, unmanned aerial vehicles (UAVs), and other payloads that could be deployed by unmanned systems. This effort needs to be more organized and guided by new operational concepts that describe how unmanned systems will contribute to undersea power projection operations and take advantage of new technologies for miniaturization of weapon guidance systems and warheads. For example, UUVs can themselves be mines or carry mines to a deployment area with today's level of sensor capability and autonomy. The Navy, however, is not aggressively developing mine payloads for UUVs and is slowly advancing the MHUV (which could likewise be a mine or carry small mines). Similarly, the Navy has experimented with small UAVs being deployed from submarines, but has not yet devised a concept for deploying them from UUVs or for using undersea-launched UAVs in power projection or surveillance operations.

These are the most significant operational concepts the Navy should be developing and analyzing as the basis behind new requirements for undersea systems. Operational concepts are essential for identifying the most important new technologies and systems to pursue, and to establish requirements for future acquisition programs.